MANAGING
PSYCHIC ABILITIES

A Real World Guide for the
Highly Sensitive Person

MANAGING PSYCHIC ABILITIES

A Real World Guide for the Highly Sensitive Person

Mary Mueller Shutan

FINDHORN PRESS

Findhorn Press
One Park Street
Rochester, Vermont 05767
www.findhornpress.com

Findhorn Press is a division of Inner Traditions International

ISBN 978-1-84409-700-5

Cataloging-in-Publication Data for this title is available from
the British Library

Printed and bound in the United States

Edited by Nicky Leach
Front cover photograph by Tulay Palaz and Kimberley Vohsen
Cover design by Richard Crookes
Text design and layout by Damian Keenan

DISCLAIMER
The information in this book is given in good faith and is neither
intended to diagnose any physical or mental condition nor to serve as a
substitute for informed medical advice or care.
Please contact your health professional for medical advice and treatment.
Neither author nor publisher can be held liable by any person for any loss
or damage whatsoever which may arise from the use of this book or any
of the information therein.

Contents

DEDICATION

Thank you to my students, many of whom were my testers for much of this material. I also wish to thank my parents who have honored my unique path, Kim Leyland and Chas Perry (who both contributed to this book, whether they realize it or not), and my husband, David, who has allowed me to fully blossom into who I am.

Thank you to those who read this, and to those of you ready to become who you fully are.

Introduction

We live in a unique time, a time in which there are now thousands of books on the market about how to develop psychic abilities. We only have to look down the block, to our largest nearby city, or online to find a school that promises to make us psychic through their classes. Reality television has a wide variety of shows focused on celebrity psychics and ghost hunters, and popular nonfiction, television, and other media suggest that we can become psychic or intuitive with relative ease. As a culture we have turned becoming more psychic or sensitive into a multi-million dollar enterprise.

It is wonderful that we live in this age. The old archetypes of the gypsy fortuneteller or the psychic as devil worshipper are fading from the forefront of our cultural narrative, and we are becoming increasingly comfortable as a society with the unexplained, the spiritual, and the psychic. Our society as a whole is evolving from one based on materialism—what can be seen, touched, and felt—to one that is both material and spiritual at the same time. Many of us want to become more sensitive, more awake, and more aware of what is going on around us on multiple levels.

But where does that leave those of us who do not want to become more psychic—who are already psychic and may not understand our sensitive natures or how to work with our abilities? We may see, sense, or feel more than the average person and feel overwhelmed. Whether we are naturally sensitive or psychic, or have developed psychic abilities, we may lack the tools to understand and work with our psychic abilities. We live in an age of interest in psychic abilities, but with the primary focus of our outer culture being on acquiring psychic abilities, there is very little information out there for those of us who may be holding on for dear life while experiencing psychic and spiritual sensitivities that we lack the capacity to deal with.

It is typical for those of us who are naturally psychic to feel overwhelmed, to not want to deal with our abilities or deny them, and to have strong emotions and experiences throughout childhood, teenage, and adult years. We may feel angry and reject the fact that we sense more than others do. We may be a part of a faith or religious path that has difficulty with sensitivities and psychic abilities, or have trauma from seeing and sensing more of the world than other people do. We may look for ways to stop the onslaught of spiritual stimuli so that we can focus on everyday ordinary existence. We seek out material not to help us develop new gifts but to manage the ones we already have.

Much of the huge range of information out there now is misinformed and not useful for those of us with already manifested psychic abilities, meaning that many of us have nowhere to turn and live life in a state of overwhelm, fear, and decreased functionality. Most spiritual communities, psychic schools, and books are aimed at aspirational psychic states, and we just do not fit into that category. There is very little information out there to support those of us who are struggling with sensitivities and psychic abilities in any real way, and society, popular media, and literature as a whole overlook the real difficulties and experiences of being a sensitive or psychic in favor of aspirational material that provides an illusion of how wonderful psychic abilities would be if we were to have them.

This book is not aimed at people who want to become psychic. There is a glut of information out there for that population. This book is the first comprehensive guide to teach people how to manage psychic abilities and sensitivities that have already manifested. As natural psychics, we do not need to learn how to become psychic; we need to understand what we are experiencing, to develop healthy boundaries with our abilities, and to learn to work with our abilities so that we can be psychic as well as functional human beings, with lives, families, and careers.

This book will help you understand the nature of psychic abilities, how they develop, and where you are on the spectrum of sensitivities and psychic abilities. Most importantly, it will teach you the basic tools and practices that will allow you to manage your psychic abilities.

Many books offer information about acquiring specific psychic abilities, such as clairvoyance (clear seeing) or clairaudience (clear hearing), but no matter how our individual sensitivities and psychic abilities manifest we all need the same basic skills to manage them. Whether we are a bit more sensitive than the average person or a highly psychic individual, we can learn how to properly take care of ourselves. This book focuses on the skills needed to manage our psychic abilities, no matter what they are. (Note: If you have interest in individual psychic abilities and how they present themselves, I suggest my first book, *The Spiritual Awakening Guide: Kun-*

dalini, Psychic Abilities, and the Conditioned Layers of Reality, for a basic overview of the different abilities and how to work with them.)

What do we mean by "managing our psychic abilities"? It can have a broad spectrum of definitions, but I understand it to mean the following: no matter our spiritual nature, or how psychic or sensitive we may be, we are intended to fully feel the wonder of our physical bodies and the joy, passion, and full range of human experiences that our lives can provide for us. We can be the most psychic or sensitive person on Earth and still learn how to work with our abilities so that we can go into even the darkest of places and come out unaffected (or minimally affected and understand what appropriate self-care is after the experience).

We are intended to have relationships, friends, and community. Many sensitives and psychics are so overwhelmed that they recede from the physical world—it is a place of overwhelm, chaos, and difficult emotions and other energies that they will have to interact with. This does not need to be the case.

Some psychics and sensitives latch onto the label of "sensitive" and assume that this means that their lives cannot contain the elements that the lives of "normal" people do. While sensitives and psychics may have a different life path in some cases, most sensitives are simply unskilled. They lack the appropriate understanding of their true nature, have not learned how to appropriately care for themselves, and do not know how to work with their abilities.

As with any tool, the more you work with your abilities, the more you will have the direct experience necessary to change your life and how you interact with your sensitivities and psychic abilities. It is possible to have a path of joy, of realizing who you are at your deepest levels, of being sensitive in a world that is not, and still being able to function at a high level. You simply have not learned how to do so yet.

Why I Developed This Work

When I was younger, I had little idea of what a psychic was. My family called me "artistic," my friends and counselors called me "sensitive," while I thought of myself as a freak who had to hide how different she was from other people in fear that they might find out that there was something wrong with me. My idea of what a psychic was at that age was the old woman who read tarot cards at the state fair or the slick psychics who appeared on talk shows. The television psychics did not represent who I was or who I wanted to be, and it was rare that one appeared truthful to me. Even if they were psychics whom I thought had abilities or were authentic, it was not as if I could call them up and ask for their advice.

On one of my first days of self-employment as a Reiki and Thai Bodywork practitioner, I finally realized what was "wrong" with me. It was one of those moments when it is abundantly and irrevocably clear what you are dealing with. I had realized that I was sensitive prior to this point, but because I was so sensitive I was consistently changing my mood, my energy, and had no concept of who I really was. I was disassociated from my physical body as a result of overwhelm, and did not respond the way many others did to stimuli such as pain, emotions, or spiritual experiences. This meant that I did not have a baseline understanding of who I was and could never really sense that something was out of the ordinary for me. This is a common issue for anyone who is highly psychic, as we will discuss later on.

But this day was different. I was thoroughly excited about my first day of work. I had two patients booked that day. The first was a Reiki session with a man who was respectful, interested, and simply stressed out because of college. He left feeling wonderful, and we both smiled at one another. Then the next person came in. He was a university professor who wanted a Thai Bodywork session. I worked on him with growing feelings of dislike, disgust, followed by hatred. After he left, I felt disgusted with myself. I was suddenly suicidal and fought off the urge to kill myself, to throw myself from the second story of the clinic room I was working in. This feeling overwhelmed me, and I could feel currents of this disgust emanating from me. I was disgusted with myself, with the world, and hated everything about myself.

I had the sudden realization that I had absorbed his feelings like a sponge. There was clearly a huge difference between the feelings of joy and excitement I had experienced with my first client that day, the happiness of a satisfied client, and the sensation of self-disgust to the point of wanting to harm myself only an hour or so later. Before that time I had no idea why I had a roller coaster of emotions constantly. I didn't know who I was, why I acted the way I did, why I had fear about simple things like going to the grocery store, why I developed odd illnesses, and why I was exhausted constantly. I simply accepted the constant changing of emotions and the fatigue as my own without question.

This single experience—of going from an almost ecstatic state of having my own business and being of service to people to being suicidal and in such darkness as if at the flick of a switch—taught me clearly that I was taking on the emotions and experiences of other people.

I left work that day and went home and began researching. Although I had been interested in chakras, meditations, mythology, the occult, psychology, and anything esoteric since I was a young child, I never could really place myself or many of my experiences prior to this realization. I just didn't know what I was looking for.

After reading hundreds of books and searching online, seeking out teachers, friends, gurus and others who could help me, I was left with some understanding of what to call myself. Empath. Clairvoyant. Clairsentient. Channel. Psychopomp. Medium. Sensitive. Clairaudient. But although all of these descriptions and words were helpful in naming what was going on with me, they didn't solve anything. They didn't teach me how to cut down on the feelings of overwhelm and fatigue I continually experienced. They didn't teach me how to control my strong psychic abilities, develop boundaries with them, or how to resolve the decades of difficult emotions and feelings of being so fundamentally different from other people.

Through the tools that I developed from various teachers, guides, and my meditation practice, I began learning how to work with and even thrive while being highly psychic. Patients who were dealing with psychic abilities increasingly began coming to see me as I learned to manage my own psychic abilities. Over the next decade, I became increasingly aware of how unskilled psychic abilities and the amount of stimuli that comes with being sensitive can create huge physical, emotional, mental, and spiritual issues. Through my work, my path, and my interactions with teachers, students, guides, spirits, and everything else in this world, I began developing programs, meditations, and resources for people dealing with psychic abilities.

I am happy that this is my path, and I love giving sensitive people (who can offer a huge amount to the world) the resources and abilities to work with their abilities without fear, to accept their gifts without anger, and to become fully functional and capable individuals.

CHAPTER ONE

How Do I Know I Have Psychic Abilities?

Imagine that four people walk into a room. The first notices fifteen things about the room and is easily able to process those fifteen things through their physical body, mind, and spirit. The second notices sixty things about the room. This person notices not only physical objects in the room but the mood of the room and the people in it. However, this person has no issue staying in a state of observing these sixty points of stimuli, and may only be conscious of twenty to forty.

The third person walks into the room. She notices one hundred and fifty pieces of information about the room. She not only notices physical objects but emotions, varying scents, even sensing the inner motivations, fears, and medical issues that the people in the room have. This is overwhelming, and she notices herself feeling slightly ill with nausea and a bit of a headache. She wants to leave and feels drained of her energy.

Person four walks into the room. He notices two thousand pieces of stimuli. Immediately he feels overwhelmed and disassociates from his physical body. There is so much information that he is unable to differentiate all of the stimuli coming in. Waves of emotion come at him, scenes like filmstrips play out before him of past happenings in the room, and everything that he sees, feels, and hears causes his nervous system to go into hyperdrive. Feelings of anxiety, fear, and dread wash over him.

In this scenario, persons one and two are noticing the normal range of stimuli and would not be considered psychic. The amount of stimuli that we see, psychic or not, is variable. We all have days where we notice more, feel more, and see more than we normally do, due to our psychology, stress level, and emotions of one day versus the next. However, we have a generally held sense of what is "normal," what most of the world can see and agrees upon seeing in our reality. Those who are within the range of normal perception, or what most other people in the room would sense, are considered non-psychic or would not be considered sensitive.

Someone who is considered sensitive or psychic is able to see, sense, feel, hear, taste, or has intuition that is beyond what is considered the normal, or agreed upon, range of perception. A psychic may have a dominant sense, or it may vary based on the situation. Like those who have a range of noticing based on day, mood, and other reasons, the psychic likewise has a variable range, and may one day be considered more in the "normal" range and other days be considered mildly psychic. This range may also create a situation where the normally highly psychic person may become so highly sensitive that they are unable to function. But all of this goes back to the elusive question of what would be considered the normal range of perception and what would be considered a deviation or heightened sensitivity from that range.

What Is Normal?

This is a difficult question in that we all consider our conditioned reality—the reality that we go about our days participating in—to be fairly concrete. We assume that when we observe the sky as being blue that others will as well. We assume that when we notice someone on the train who is a bit odd that others are seeing him as well. The fact that we have an objective, observable reality is what we base our scientific endeavors on, and how we feel confident that the reality we observe is in fact real.

But this is not true by any measure. It is well known to police officers, for example, that two people can observe a crime from the same vantage point at the same time and recall the events that transpired totally differently. One person may say that the perpetrator was Hispanic, in his forties, with dark thick hair and a sparse beard. The other person may say that the perpetrator was Irish, in his thirties, with thinning light brown hair and a thick beard. Even when observing the same crime the two individuals, who would not be considered sensitive or psychic, give different accounts of the same reality. So even in normalcy, where people are fully participating in ordinary reality—the reality that we all think that we can agree upon—we all see, feel, and think different things when faced with the same exact scenario.

Moreover, in the normal range of perception, we still have dominant senses and dominant ways that we process information. One person may notice smells, another may process things visually, and another may recall spoken words. This is all within what is considered normal range of behavior and processing of events. We are all unique individuals (even those of us who are considered within the normal range of perception) who see, think, feel, touch, and taste things differently. What is more, we all have "filters":

beliefs and past experiences that color our reality. If we have never experienced something, we are less likely to believe it is real. Although a difficult subject to broach, all of us have biases and filters that cause us to notice different things about the world. Simply put, there is a reason that one person noticed a perpetrator as Irish and the other noticed him as Hispanic.

In considering the normal or non-psychic, there are, of course, variations, dominant senses, and abilities to perceive that cover the whole range of the human, sensate experience. If we were to look at the basic definition of non-psychic, it would be a person who sees, feels, hears, and participates in reality the way that the vast majority of people do and within a normal range of perception. They are on the normal range of noticing stimuli—meaning that they walk into a room and notice things that are in the typical range of perception, or that many of the people who walk into that room would perceive.

If you were to walk them into a room, many non-psychics would notice the same ten to fifteen things about it. They may also pick up unspoken energies, such as sexual attraction, and be aware of the chemistry, general charisma, and magnetism of some people in the room. Subconscious information will allow them to know not to go up to a specific person because they will bore them, or will cause them to feel inexplicably drawn to a person in that room without knowing why.

Our first impressions of people as leaders, our impression of someone in a job interview, as alpha or beta-type males, as strong independent women versus dependent women are picked up by the normal range of perception. Both non-psychics and psychics rely on this information every day to allow them to understand who to have relationships with, who to hire, and who to stay away from. Even if we consider ourselves the densest, least psychic, and most scientifically oriented person on Earth, our intuition and the subconscious information we pick up about our environment informs our decisions and our general lives. The psychic simply has a higher degree of receiving and possibility of understanding more non-physical, non-material stimuli, and of having that material become conscious (or apparent to them).

Both the non-psychic and psychic vary in which days they notice stimuli. On a Wednesday, for example, the non-psychic may be able to name five things in the room and not notice any emotional overtones to the room, whereas on a Friday, they may be able to name twenty things in the room and an emotion or two present in the room, as well as subconscious stimuli. This is completely natural and is based on individual energy levels, emotions, and even greater fluctuations, such as the menstrual cycle in women.

Psychics also have variable abilities and a range in what they notice. And as with the non-psychic, these are individual fluctuations based on everything from our energy levels, hormones, moon cycle, emotions, and psychology to the amount of stimuli that is present in a place. If we say that the general range of conscious noticing for a non-psychic is five to twenty points of stimuli and subconsciously is a range of fifteen to one hundred points of stimuli, then the psychic would notice twenty to two thousand points of stimuli consciously and one hundred to two hundred thousands points of stimuli subconsciously. Since there are no double-blind tests that can show how much material we subconsciously pick up, these numbers are somewhat arbitrary and are being used for illustration purposes only.

Non-psychic as well as psychic individuals must process the conscious as well as subconscious stimuli coming at them—mentally, emotionally, energetically, and physically.

When we think of psychic or other stimuli (emotional, energetic, spiritual), we tend to consider it as being "nonphysical," meaning that we typically think someone who is psychic has the ability to "see beyond" into spiritual realms. But being psychic simply means that you are more sensitive and able to pick up stimuli such as emotions, thoughts, ideas, weather patterns, health issues, or more information about a vase on a table than other people would see or sense.

Our current archetype of what we consider to be a "psychic" has been obscured and mystified in order to fit a specific cultural paradigm, which leaves real psychics struggling and not understanding their abilities and how to work with them. In reality, there are different ways that we are sensitive or psychic. Someone who is sensitive may not be in contact with the spirit world, but they may notice thirty-five things about a lamp while most people notice one or two things about it. If we realize that the words "sensitive" or "psychic" just means that we notice more than the average person, this should help demystify the word and the complex cultural narrative we have formulated around it.

We are a continuum of energy. Our spiritual, emotional, mental, and physical natures are not separate. In simple terms, this means that no matter how much stimuli we receive and process each day, we do so not only spiritually but also emotionally, mentally, and physically. The non-psychic who has to only consciously process ten items in the room, and subconsciously thirty items, will have much less to "digest" than the sensitive who walks into the room and notices thirty items consciously and four hundred subconsciously.

This is a lot for a person to take in, and one of the calling cards of an unskilled psychic is fatigue, digestive upset, headaches or migraines, heart issues, and a state of overwhelm, as such people lack the ability to sort and properly process the overwhelming stimuli coming their way. This is similar to how a non-psychic person who ordinarily has ten items on their "to-do" list suddenly having a week where they have multiple things to do at work, with their children, as well as having their in-laws coming into town, will feel the effects of having too much information to process as well.

To summarize: a non-psychic is someone who participates within a "normal" range of noticing and processing of stimuli. Someone outside of that range would be considered psychic. But it's important to state that even in the normal ranges of human perception, there is a great deal of variation, and what we consider to be concrete, conditioned reality is actually quite subjective.

Psychics themselves vary greatly in their abilities, what they notice, and their skill set, ranging from the mildly psychic person who is open to receiving and noticing their gut intuition and more of the subconscious stimuli of a room to someone who is highly sensitive and receiving huge amounts of information that is way beyond the range of normal human perception. In Chapter Two, we will examine in greater detail the differences between levels of sensitivity, from one end of the spectrum (someone who may notice a few more items in that room than the average person) to the other (someone who is highly psychic and would notice a huge amount of information about that room, subconsciously and consciously).

Many psychic abilities, especially strong ones, run in families and have ancestral and genetic roots or causes. Depending on the family, such psychics may be able to learn how to properly work with their abilities and develop boundaries with them through a similarly minded and understanding parent or relative.

But even when psychic abilities do run in families there is a tendency toward persecution, a culture of not talking about abilities, or even a hatred of psychic abilities that has developed due to emotional traumas endured by members of the family who have struggled with being psychic or a genetic history of ancestors being persecuted, locked up, or even put to death due to their abilities or sensitivities. Even if they allow the person with abilities to be of service in some way to humanity, many religions to this day consider psychic abilities to be an affront to the Lord or a tool of the devil. This obviously puts a huge strain on the psychic, who is likely unskilled and struggling with not only how to deal with their abilities but also persecution from their church, religious communities, and families concerning their psychic abilities.

Other psychics have spent years seeking out teachers, developing inner guidance, and relying on a variety of books, non-physical guides, and life experiences to develop the tools to become skilled at working with their abilities. But the vast majority of natural psychics are unskilled, meaning that they lack the proper knowledge and tools to work with their abilities and develop boundaries with them, and may be in a state of denial or lack acceptance of their sensitivity level.

Unskilled Versus Skilled

Skilled psychics understand that they are sensitive, have accepted this to the degree that they are willing to work with their psychic abilities, and have the proper tools and understandings to be a functional yet psychic human being. Functionality is of importance, as we live in a modern world and we all need to go to the grocery store, develop relationships with others, and thrive as human beings, even if we are having psychic and spiritual experiences.

This functionality may be different from our non-psychic counterparts. We may still find the emotions in a grocery store difficult, require certain tools and preparation time to go to the hospital, or still find ourselves in a place of wanting simple, non-chaotic interactions and experiences. We may enjoy and require solitude, find solace in animals, and have difficulty watching the news or participating online. There may be days that we are overwhelmed with a wave or influx of extrasensory information. We may have health issues due to our sensitivity levels.

In spite of this, the skilled psychic typically has the tools to be functional. Although we may not choose to go to a bar, we have the resources to do so, if necessary. We can know how to take care of ourselves after going to a hospital, or other place with heavy or difficult energy. There may be some days or hours in which the amount of psychic information coming at us causes us to become ill or nonfunctional, but most days are functional and healthy. Our definition of functionality may be different from those who are non-psychic, but the skilled psychic will be able to fully express their humanness and develop friendships, follow their life path, and have a career.

Skilled psychics may have different lives, different career paths, and choose different ways to interact, due in part to their sensitivities. But although they may live a life that is different from the typical trajectory, that does not mean that they are dysfunctional or do not understand how to work with their abilities. Many skilled psychics are unable to work in environments that do not suit their abilities. They are closer to their truth and the idea of working in a career that does not suit them, or a typical nine-to-five job, might sound horrible to them. They may choose one-on-one interactions and be brilliant counselors, healers, writers, painters, and so on, but unable to work in an office building in a cubicle. It is common for even the skilled psychic to have to come to terms with the fact that their lives may have a different path from the non-psychic, and to have to reconcile societal expectations of normalcy.

The above relates to moderate to high psychic abilities. Someone with basic sensitivities or some psychic abilities is likely to just need a few skills to be healthier and more interactive in their lives. Generally, the more psychic we are, the more aware we are, and the more difficult it is to keep with typical societal norms. This is because no matter our skill level, we simply notice, sense, and feel more, which may cause us to question or have difficulty with what is expected of us culturally or societally. This can lead to interesting but sometimes difficult interactions with others and the world.

To summarize, skilled psychics are people who:

- have the proper tools to work with their abilities;
- have boundaries;
- know how to protect themselves, if necessary;
- have a regular spiritual hygiene routine;
- can open or shut down their abilities;
- are able to properly process the large amount of stimuli coming at them;
- have the ability to understand and differentiate the different stimuli and psychospiritual experiences they encounter;
- are in control of their abilities, their surroundings, and their experiences in this world;
- have worked through the trauma of being different to come to a state of loving acceptance of themselves and their sensitivities.

In contrast, the unskilled psychic may lack the ability or desire to learn about their sensitivities, has difficulties dealing with them, has issues with functionality, and is in a state of overwhelm due to their abilities. This is especially evident with stronger psychic abilities and advanced psychic states.

The unskilled psychic feels out of control—fearful, angry, and perhaps desperate about what they are experiencing. While the skilled psychic is (mostly, if not fully) in the driver's seat and can control, guide, and work with their experiences, the unskilled psychic consistently feels as if things are happening *to* them. They feel victimized by their sensitivities. While the unskilled psychic may have some idea that they are sensitive, they lack the ability to catalogue or understand their experiences.

Unskilled psychics lack boundaries and are unable to protect themselves from an onslaught of psychic stimuli coming their way. Frequently, unskilled psychics experience difficulties with health, especially digestive difficulties and conditions associated with exhaustion, as well as nervous system, heart, and immune issues. They often feel cloudy, not themselves, or lack the mental acuity or concentration fully needed for their day. There are emotional issues as well as a variety of traumas associated with being sensitive, and a feeling of something being really wrong. It is common for sensitives to see themselves as "freaks" or different and for them to not know why they relate to or understand the world differently or on such a deep level. There is a tendency toward addictions and behavior that shuts down or anesthetizes the unskilled psychic from feeling or sensing too much. There is hesitation in telling others about sensitivities or psychic abilities for fear of being judged by others.

As far as we have come as a culture, there is still a lack of acknowledgment about sensitivities, and psychics can go through counseling, hospitalization, and receive medication, all of which are only somewhat helpful unless the psychic also learns the appropriate tools to manage their psychic sensitivities. The word "psychic" carries a lot of weight in our culture, and it is normal for people to not wish to identify as being psychic, or to deny being psychic due to religious, family, or cultural representations of psychics. While this has eased a bit, the subject of acceptance of sensitivities and psychic abilities in a world in which most people are not sensitive can be a difficult subject to heal for the psychic or sensitive. When someone is able to accept their psychic abilities and sensitivities, they are better able to manage them.

If we were to re-establish the word "psychic" as simply meaning someone who notices more than what is considered "normal" reality, or the normal range of human perception, there would likely be more comfort with the term, and more people would be willing to accept that they are psychic. But due to our complex cultural heritage and the word being associated with aspirational psychic books, scam artists, and "woo-woo" sorts, there is a stereotype present that is hard to move beyond. If we were to understand that the following are all examples of psychics in our culture—the top detective on the police force who notices minute traces of blood and can tell when people are lying, the housewife who has the gut reaction of when one of her children is in danger, and the artist who creates otherworldly paintings—we can move beyond those stereotypes to fully understand that psychics and sensitives can present in many different ways.

With the unskilled psychic there are always difficulties, but the amount of difficulties varies from mild to completely dysfunctional. This variation is due to the strength of the psychic abilities (how psychic you are) but also the emotional and physical background of the individual experiencing them. A history of trauma and abuse in a mildly psychic person may cause extreme difficulties with daily functioning and managing of psychic abilities while a moderately psychic individual with no trauma background may have only slight difficulties.

It is always true that highly sensitive and unskilled psychics, no matter their personal backgrounds, nearly always have physical, emotional, mental, and spiritual difficulties as long as they lack the tools they need to properly work with their abilities. There is a certain tipping point at which the amount of stimuli coming at people who are highly psychic is so strong that unless they have the proper understandings they will be constantly in a state of overwhelm.

They also have difficulty emotionally accepting their psychic abilities and sensitivities. This is true for both men and women, although some men certainly have more difficulty accepting any type of sensitivity due to the cultural constraints of men needing to be strong and non-sensitive. It is frequently true that it will take years, if not decades, for the psychic to accept that what they are experiencing may be due to spiritual or psychic causes.

It may take even longer for the unskilled psychic to accept their abilities enough to be willing to seek out books, information online, or a proper teacher. Frequently, when we get to this point, there is additional frustration in finding that 99 percent of materials out there are for aspirational psychics and subsequent difficulty in finding a teacher who actually can help them. Since most of the schools and books are for aspirational psychics, the graduates then call themselves "psychic" simply because they have graduated from a specific program, typically becoming teachers of the school and going out into the community representing themselves as psychics. These "psychics" may or may not actually be psychic, or skilled, or able to help the actual or natural psychic in any way.

Real Versus Fake

Although understandably a difficult and controversial subject, the subject of "real" versus "fake" in the psychic arena certainly needs to be broached. Technically, we can all become more psychic than we are right now by noticing more of our surroundings. We all can learn how to scan rooms, consciously remember more material, and learn to read some of the subconscious emotions and energies of people, places, and things.

In fact, most of the population should do this very thing. They should discover more of their inner landscape, their motivations, what makes them tick. They should notice things outside themselves—notice the world that surrounds them and learn to read people so that they can interact on a deeper level. Everyone should learn to be more sensitive to other people's needs, learn how to read situations to tell if they are in danger, be able to figure out if they should be interacting in a different way with people in the office or out in the world. Developing compassion and interest in the world around us is a vital part of becoming more awake and sensitive human beings. It can only lead to good to be able to consider other thoughts, people, and to become more sensitive overall. If all of us were to become more sensitive to the point that we can consider more than ourselves, and our own beliefs and reality to be the only valid truth, this world would be a much more peaceful and healed place.

We have established that psychic simply means to notice more than the average person, or to notice beyond what is considered to be a rather fixed and arbitrary version of reality. Under this definition we can all become more "psychic" than we are right now. However, there is a clear differentiation between fake and real psychic abilities.

A "fake" psychic may actually be a rather harsh way of describing someone who is mildly or moderately psychic but presenting that they are highly psychic, either out of ignorance or to make a career for themselves. So the first definition of a "fake" psychic is someone who exaggerates his or her skills and abilities. They may do this because they have never met anyone that is more sensitive than they are, because they have read a few aspirational books, have attended a school for psychics and are now certified as a psychic, or because they are simply more psychic than they were before.

It is also typical for some people to develop an interest in psychic abilities through watching television shows and reading books and to determine that they are sensitive, not realizing that there are broad spectrums of psychic sensitivities and they are on the lower end of the spectrum. This is entirely understandable, as many of us simply have not interacted with other psychics, and the illusions provided by watching television psychics, reading aspirational books, or interacting online with other people much like ourselves, are not likely to present us with a different reality.

This is the biggest representation of "psychic" in popular media and society: the mild to moderate psychic. This is the person who proudly announces that they are psychic, calls into police stations with tips about dreams they had, and goes up to people in grocery stores saying that they have their dead grandmother with them. There is a lack of understanding in this "fake" category that psychic skills are variable on a day-to-day basis and that we do not have all of the answers. This sense of ego and inflated sense of self-importance turns the people in this category into "fakes" because they are misrepresenting themselves and their abilities.

It is important in any spiritual path to have integrity and honesty. It is also important to realize how much you do not know. Being psychic, even mildly psychic, opens us up to the hidden, the not typically seen. This can be a wonderful thing, but it can also create a situation in which simply because we know a bit more than our non-psychic neighbor we assume that we know everything. We will make up facts and psychic manifestations out of our own egos instead of simply stating that we do not know, or that we are not receiving information. One of my teachers used to say that you could tell someone who knew a little something by how loudly they shouted that they knew everything. This personifies this first category of "fake" psychic.

This first category represents the vast majority of psychics in popular culture. Many genuine psychics do not identify with such individuals. As we've noted, people in this first category may have a mild to moderate capability to see, feel, hear, and notice beyond. However, because of how they are presenting themselves, and because most of the material they come up with is self-generated—the result of clever acting, and not of interacting with any real spiritual forces or being able to read deeply into a room or person—it is considered to be in the "fake" category.

The truth is that if you are a medium, it is rare for people to appear at whim; if you are psychic, most paying customers want to hear pleasant lies rather than anything a real highly skilled psychic may want to say. The ability of the "fake" psychic to work out what the person wants to hear and who they may want to talk to using basic psychological constructs, Google searches, and asking questions, results in minimally talented or able psychics making up the vast majority of working psychics and the psychics we are most likely to encounter on television, the internet, and in the school or shop on the corner.

There are clear reasons why "fake" psychics are so clearly represented in the media and are able to make careers for themselves. This is based off of the psychological needs of the client rather than the psychic having any sensitivities or spiritual capabilities. If someone is visiting a medium to hear from their dead son and wants to hear that they are okay, but hears from someone with high-level sensitivities that their great-aunt Myrtle is coming through instead, and that their son doesn't wish to talk, then this is clearly something that they would not want to hear. However, if a "fake" psychic says that their son loves and forgives them, which is what the person wants and needs to psychologically hear, they walk away with what they want or expect out of the psychic.

Another simple example is that of the popular tarot card reader doing a reading on someone's relationship. Most people want to hear from their tarot reader that their boyfriend (or girlfriend) isn't cheating on them, and the fake psychic is much more likely to say that they are not, and to tell them what they wish to hear about the relationship is what they see. A psychic who can actually see into the situation will likely see that the partner is cheating, and has the choice of telling the person and possibly not getting a tip, or lying and saying everything is wonderful. Our relationship with psychic abilities is certainly complex; there is a reason why there is a glut of minimally sensitive psychics with well-established careers out there, successful in equal part due to their understanding of human psychology and their own charisma and acting abilities.

The second category of "fake" psychics are truly fakes. They are actors who have very limited or no abilities and are simply out to make money. This can be a very lucrative career for a person with the right pitch and thousands of books as well as motivational speakers and others have whole programs on how to become psychic in six easy steps, how to easily raise your kundalini, or how to become a medium in a month. Countless others do séances, clear houses, work with spirits, and claim to be mediums or offer other psychic capabilities for money. While many truly talented psychics are drawn to helping and working with people, the truly fake psychics frequently have exorbitant fees and have a specific look or personality based on giving a packaged presentation of being psychic with little actual substance.

A wide variety of scams and issues are associated with these practitioners—everything from setting up devices to create knocking sounds on tables to telling customers that they have a curse placed on them that will take thousands of dollars to remove. Some of these psychics are predatory and out to make a buck out of gullible and frequently troubled customers.

There is a long and rather interesting history of this type of behavior. In this case, the psychic not only self-generates or creates an environment of giving the customer exactly what they want or what they want to hear but sets up fake customers in the audience to read, places mechanisms in a room to create sounds or mists, or uses intimidation to convince others that their deceased loved ones are in trouble or stuck and they are the only one who can fix it. In some cases, practitioners will outright claim to curse people who do not pay them money. Most people in this category know nothing about what being psychic actually entails and simply follow the scripts from movies, from the schools they have attended, and what they have seen through books and television shows.

The last category of fake psychic is that of the "ego-based psychic." This of course is evident in the other groups but deserves its own category because it clearly shows the difference between a fake versus a real psychic. The ego-based psychic is convinced that they know the totality of the cosmos. Their opinion is always right, and no matter their psychic ability or advancement, they are the most highly skilled and the most advanced psychic out there. Everyone else is inferior to them.

In a session they are always able to do and say exactly what someone may want from them. If you want your dead Aunt Sally to come through, she does. If you want to hear that your boyfriend will come back to you, of course he will. If you want to hear that you should sell all of your belongings and move to Thailand, this will be the reading that you get. These sorts claim that they know everything that happens after death, in the spiritual realms, or even in the cosmos. They do this to fulfill your secret wishes, desires, and needs. Many of these types of practitioners do not realize that they are predatory, but the sort of behavior that causes someone to believe that they know the totality of the cosmos is based in ego. Any highly or even moderately psychic individual will tell you that there is no way to know the totality of the cosmos, to have control over it, or to know exactly what goes on after death or in other realms.

In the modern day, we also have fake psychics who are taking on the role of guru. While some psychics, such as medical intuitives, can certainly pick up on health information, and there certainly are people who channel a wide variety of energies, there is now a wide variety of psychic and sensitive "gurus" who claim that they channel Jesus, or can tell you everything you want to know about your health, often with exorbitant fees.

Upon examination, most of these "channels" and health "gurus" are revealing little more than plant-based diets or health information that any first-year medical or nutrition student would know. These people will be predatory, often saying that they and only they contain such knowledge that they have to offer, creating a system in which desperate individuals offer up a lot of money that they do not have to the guru. Meanwhile, a much less expensive visit to a holistic health practitioner with actual training, such as a Naturopath, Acupuncturist, or experienced Herbalist would have gotten them much farther along their path.

Some of the ego-based practitioners may actually be psychic in some manner. Anyone who actually is psychic knows that most people desire comfort over actual spiritual readings or understandings. They want to hear that their dead Aunt Sally is okay and forgives them. They don't want to hear that she didn't come through or that she is still earth-bound because she is really upset. People do not want to hear that their relationship is doomed, or that you are much better off staying at your job and with your family rather than moving to Bali.

Many psychics who are professionals respect and work with this fact. They have to make a living, and many of them simply can't afford to tell you that your cousin isn't coming through or things that you do not want to hear, because there would be a small percentage of repeat customers. People want to hear that you, and only you, have specific knowledge of the cosmos, or whatever area of expertise the psychic is claiming. But this is not how psychic abilities work, or how they manifest.

The truth is that psychic abilities are highly variable and the totality of the spiritual realms and the cosmos are not available to someone simply because they are psychic. They also are not available to just one person. More than that, being psychic does not mean that you know everything.

This is the number one thing to watch out for in terms of psychics. Any psychic who is highly sensitive and skilled will know that they know some things, but that the spiritual realms are a large place and they will never know everything, and what they know today might be totally different tomorrow. True psychics know that not everything has an answer, and are able to freely admit when they do not know things. They are able to tell people when they are having an "off" day and will typically reschedule, or know far enough in advance to not schedule clients on that day. They will tell people what actually comes through for you, instead of catering to what you want to hear, see, or know. The client may want their mother to come through and instead their next-door neighbor does, or nobody does at all. The psychic may also be having an "off" day and not able to perceive something that another psychic who is having an on day or simply more skilled or highly psychic would notice.

As with any line of work, professional psychics have specific interests and capabilities. They may be able to see love and how relationships work but not anything about mediumship or death. Skilled, professional psychics who fit into the "real" category will know what their capabilities and interests are and will refer you out to another psychic if they feel someone else would be a better fit or is more advanced or skilled in a certain area than they are.

In the general population, fake psychics abound. It is more obvious with professionals, but the same categories appear. Ego-based, mildly or moderately talented psychics populate chat rooms, are our friends, and are in our communities. Many of these people mean no harm, and are truly ignorant of the fact that there are others that receive much more stimuli than they do. Many people simply have no understanding that there are actually people out there who are psychic naturally or who have strong psychic abilities. It is generally a "grass is always greener" syndrome wherein people with mild abilities will be interested in becoming psychic and will call themselves psychic and those with stronger abilities will want to shut down their abilities, have difficulties with them, have a long struggle to accept them, and may have difficulty with the word "psychic" or referring to themselves as such. This is true of most natural and strong real psychics until they get the skills and understandings to work with their abilities and have them be not such a detriment to their existence.

A general understanding of most "real" psychics is that there are always more out there than we can possibly fathom. Beyond the fact that there are always going to be people that notice different things or simply notice more in the environment, thus making them more psychic, a real psychic understands that there are always things that we may be ignorant of.

Psychic abilities are filtered through our very human bodies, and we resonate with experiences, stimuli, and visions of what we have known before. Put simply, two psychics of an equally sensitive nature may walk into a room and one of them notices that someone who inhabited the room in the past was a victim of domestic violence and the other picks up that a former pet is buried in the back yard. This means that a real psychic is unable to promise specific results or that they will pick up specific things. If a stimulus is very strong, it is likely that both psychics will notice it, but like the example of two non-psychics witnessing a crime and giving different accounts, psychic abilities are also perceived through the filter of experience, as well as the additional abilities of skill and openness.

As we have discussed, a real psychic is unable to promise to deliver specific messages or results. Like most people, psychics have days where they are quite sensitive as well as days of cloudiness and lower abilities to perceive. True psychics are unable to present your deceased daughter to you because she may simply not come through that day or the psychic may be having a bad day and is unable to perceive her. Human variables, such as physical sickness or spiritual imbalance, may mean that the psychic, although genuine, may be unable to perceive much of anything.

Ideally, the psychic would come to a state of balance with their abilities and be able to open and close them at will. This can occur in a highly skilled state, but since psychic abilities and sensitivities are not only a result of the individual psychic and their physical, mental, and emotional health but also what may be going on in the community, in the world, and even in the cosmos, there is to some degree a loss of control of when and to what degree even the most highly skilled, advanced psychic can promise to be able to use their skills.

Real psychics are very much aware of this fact, and in fact many ethical professional psychics will change around their appointments or simply take a sick day or time for self-nurturing when they know that they are going to have an "off" day. Skilled psychics learn to perceive when "off" days are going to occur, often knowing in advance when they might need a few hours, a day, or even a week off.

Even for the most skilled psychic, it is difficult to control the amount of psychic material coming in and the opening and closing of psychic capabilities. While the false psychic maintains that they can control their abilities at all times, the true psychic understands that they can only control psychic stimuli and spiritual happenings to a certain degree. Even the most highly skilled, highly sensitive psychic will know to leave a place that is overwhelming and to protect themselves and draw boundaries when necessary.

In simple terms, a true psychic understands that they cannot control or know everything, and that there will be times when they know less and are completely overwhelmed or not able to control much of anything. They respect and are humble about their sensitivities and do not pretend to know or be more than they are. They understand that however much they know, there are others who know much more than they do and understand that they do not know the totality of the cosmos.

That being said, while most ethical true psychics will be honest in their actions and readings, as business people professional psychics may tell clients what they want to hear instead of what they are actually sensing so as to have a profitable business or because they do not wish to inflict pain on their clients. Ideally, a true psychic would be honest and ethical in all of their dealings, but since "psychic" has become a business, even those who are truly psychic may succumb to viable business practices rather than higher truth of what they sense. In this situation, the customer may not be ready or open enough to truly hear what the psychic has to say, and most professional, business-savvy psychics have to create a delicate balance of saying what comes through and what the client is ready to listen to.

Most true psychics have been psychic from a very young age, generally since birth. All children are open and sensitive, but the psychic child can be so highly psychic that adults are able to pinpoint there being something strange or atypical about the child.

The psychic child, if not traumatized, will become a psychic adult with a blossoming or opening of abilities during the teenage years or early adulthood. The traumatized psychic child who is told that they are atypical and that it is not appropriate to have imaginary friends or be psychic past a certain age will cut off their abilities until they are safe to emerge again. They may also put on a mask to fit in with their schoolmates and families and only let their psychic abilities emerge in private.

If a psychic child shuts down their abilities, the emergence can come at any age and may not have the strength of their childhood abilities, due to a variety of factors. Typically, most highly psychic individuals are genetically predisposed, meaning that it comes through their family lineage. There are many reasons why psychic abilities develop, but the strongest cases of "true" psychics are either a result of genetic predisposition or trauma, or both.

CHAPTER TWO

Why Psychic Abilities Develop

A person's natural psychic abilities, especially if they are strong, have typically been present since birth or early childhood. People who manifest the strongest abilities are hereditary psychics, meaning that someone or several people in the familial line are psychic. In some families this is well known—there are great traditions of soothsayers and oracles who train their unskilled children to become skilled psychics.

But in many families, members with psychic abilities are relegated to the role of the strange aunt that nobody talks about or a family member who may have been medicated or institutionalized for being crazy. It is typical for very strong psychics to have several generations of family members who were psychic, may or may not want to admit their sensitivities, or know how to deal with their abilities. In some lucky cases, a living family member can teach them how to work with their abilities. This is an ideal situation, because psychic abilities present very differently in each person but seem to manifest rather similarly in family members.

Our childhoods have a huge impact on how we see the world. People who have endured severe or moderate childhood abuse and trauma are more sensitive. This is a basic biological survival mechanism that was enacted during an abuse cycle in order to simply survive. When we were children we had to notice more, see more, hear more, feel more, because it allowed us to survive a difficult situation that we could not escape.

When we are under periods of stress, our nervous systems trigger our ability to notice more stimuli in our environment. Since our childhoods shape and develop the way we see the world, this trauma response creates a highly sensitive and psychic child. Since much of the programming that is developed in early childhood follows us for the rest of our lives, trauma in infancy and early childhood leads us to notice more stimuli and to become more sensitive or psychic.

If trauma continues over a period of time during our teenage or adult years (during wartime, for example), it can lead to what is known as post-traumatic stress disorder (PTSD) as well as increased sensitivity. Sudden trauma, such as from a near-death experience, can also create a rapid expansion of sensitivity. Anyone who has experienced trauma must learn to take responsibility for their emotional balance and learn how to regulate their nervous system, in addition to acquiring tools to manage their psychic abilities. Psychics who fall into other categories will also have to work through difficult emotions, but for them, the highest priority may not be emotional but instead involve learning boundaries and other spiritual skills.

In some cases, psychic abilities seem to manifest spontaneously. When looking back it is typical that there is an event that created this, either as in the example of a near-death experience, severe illness, or even something as simple as a death in the family. Dealing with events that put us into greater touch with our spiritual natures, or something bigger than ourselves, can be a trigger for the spontaneous emergence of psychic abilities.

Many of us report a feeling of expansion with peak experiences, such as after a certain amount of miles running or exercising in other ways, such as skydiving or hiking through a particular place in nature. Although for most of us these experiences are temporary, for some they are a trigger for latent psychic abilities. These include abilities expressed in childhood but closed down for fear of what the larger culture may think and ancestral and genetic abilities that remain or begin opening.

In other cases, psychic abilities emerge after taking part in specific classes, meditations, prayers, or trainings. Such activities may create a situation of mild or sometimes moderate psychic abilities. Meditation retreats as well as courses in Reiki or Shamanic Healing may allow temporary enhancement of abilities, or an increase in their expression; this typically lasts for the duration of the course and for a short time afterward. Most of us, unless we have an at-home practice or are engaged in a larger spiritual process, will remain in the mild psychic abilities range and will end up seeking more classes, workshops, and communities to repeat our experiences or enhance our abilities.

Spiritual awakenings, such as kundalini awakenings, open the psychic centers as a byproduct of a larger spiritual process. This is also true of religious awakenings, wherein someone engaged in religious practices such as devotion and prayer has a direct experience with God or feels the Holy Spirit. In this case, spiritual abilities can manifest quickly and strongly but are part of a larger spiritual process.

Psychic abilities naturally develop and grow stronger the closer we are to an awakened state. It is part of the path. Traditionally, people strived for *siddhis* (essentially, psychic abilities or tricks showing psychic abilities) to amass followers and show others how far down the spiritual path they were. In spiritual awakenings, it is easy for people to get wrapped up in developing spiritual capabilities such as psychic powers and stop their progress into a truly awakened state. Psychic abilities and greater noticing of the world around us naturally emerges on a deep spiritual path. Rather than be the focus or end point of our path, these capabilities can allow us to progress farther along our path.

In rare cases, psychic abilities and sensitivities can appear seemingly because they were meant to happen. For such individuals, there is no pattern of abuse in early childhood, no sudden expansion of awareness due to ongoing or sudden trauma in our lifetime, no genetic predisposition toward sensitivities. Although this category is certainly less prevalent and typically has milder manifestations than the others, some of us were born into this life with sensitivities because of a job we are intended to pursue or a path we should follow. Some psychics are great dancers, writers, teachers, healers, social workers, and so on and are meant to bring their sensitivities to a certain portion of the world at a specific time.

In many cases of genetic predisposition, there is an original trauma trigger. Descendants of those caught up in wars and genocides and those of us from countries that are repeatedly torn apart by politics and other upheavals may exhibit what is known as ancestral trauma. An ancestor of ours at some point may have needed to be in a state of alertness, readiness, and of observing more about their environment. In this case, the original trauma has created the pattern and way of being due to an ancestor, which has then been passed down through the generations.

There are some other reasons for psychic abilities, such as rare examples of past lives creating psychic abilities, although this can usually be traced to one of the other categories. Some forms of energy work, magic and occult practices, and religious practices can create psychic abilities and other psychic and spiritual phenomena. Traditionally, those who became strong psychics typically would be considered to "have the gift," meaning that they are genetically predisposed to strong psychic abilities. In some cultures, children who are born with the caul still intact, or who have specific birthmarks, are thought to be psychic. Many people with latent psychic abilities that they turned off in childhood are subconsciously drawn to activities such as shamanic journeying, occult practices, spiritual paths, meditation, and other pursuits as a way to turn their natural abilities from childhood back on.

It is quite common for someone to have a mixture of the above categories. For example, someone with natural psychic abilities in their family line may suffer in early childhood as a result of a parent who has empathic abilities but does not know how to work with the emotions coming in and gets angry and drinks. Others of us may feel as if there is a genetic component to our psychic abilities but not know if this is actually true. It can be enormously helpful to have an understanding of where our psychic abilities come from in order to understand how they may similarly manifest in ourselves and become skilled in our own gifts.

Most of us are not fortunate enough to have a living relative skilled in psychic abilities, but we may be aware of others in our ancestry who had such abilities, or with knowledge of basic psychology, suspect that the trauma we endured as children made us more sensitive to the world. When it comes down to it, though, if we do not have a living relative who has taught us about our psychic abilities, or we are unaware that we are sensitive, we are grasping at straws in our understanding of our abilities.

The Sensitive

It is typical that people who are sensitive were told throughout their childhoods that being sensitive was somehow wrong or inappropriate. People are often told to "stop being so sensitive" if they exhibit a sensitive or more feeling nature, and came to negatively associate their sensitive natures with being overly emotional, or exhibiting aberrant, "non-normal" behavior.

It is not unusual for highly sensitive people to have a long history of medical complaints, such as digestion issues, headache, fatigue, heart palpitations, depression or moods swings and other emotional complaints, and difficulty in crowds, schools, and social situations. Many children and teenagers who are highly sensitive endure psychiatric evaluations, medications, and hospitalizations seeking to change them into someone who is considered normal and can fit into schools, can achieve adolescent milestones, and get along with their peers more readily.

In 1996, the psychological construct of the "Highly Sensitive Person" was established by Elaine Aron and offered a revolutionary step forward. It created identifying markers or an archetype of the Highly Sensitive Person that has helped lead to acceptance of the sensitive person within the context of mainstream psychology and culture. The basic definition of a Highly Sensitive Person is someone who is more aware of his or her surroundings and is often overwhelmed when they are in a highly stimulated environment. Aron's work helped establish being sensitive as something that is common enough that it can be considered a character trait, a type of personality found to some degree in about 15-20 percent of the population.

Degrees of psychic ability vary greatly in highly sensitive people, so it's useful to break this down a bit. Being highly sensitive and having psychic abilities are on a continuum. As we discussed earlier, this is the difference between the psychic who walks into a room and notices twenty sources of stimuli and one that notices two thousand. Someone who is highly sensitive, can read people fairly well, and decides to be a counselor or nurse but remains functional throughout their day is on one end of the continuum, while someone who is highly psychic to the degree that they are constantly inundated by spirits and take on others' emotions to the point that they lose themselves and are not able to function properly in the world is on the other end of the continuum. This continuum would then be broken down into segments of the sensitive population, including highly sensitive, mildly psychic, moderately psychic, and highly psychic individuals.

Most highly sensitive and mildly psychic individuals experience little difficulty with their greater ability to notice things and, as discussed earlier, are often in the aspirational category, meaning they have an active interest in developing their abilities or wish to have them be stronger or more open.

A small percentage of the population would fit into the moderate psychic ability range. And a very small percentage of psychics would be considered highly psychic. For example in a room full of 1,000 people, four may be moderately psychic and one may be considered highly psychic. However, you are not likely to find a moderately or highly psychic person in a room full of that many people unless they have to be—it's just too overwhelming.

Moderately and highly psychic individuals typically have more difficulty with the sheer amount of stimuli coming their way and with knowing how to integrate their psychic experiences while functioning on a daily basis. They often will consider their abilities to be a curse rather than a gift, and will have greater difficulty finding resources, a peer group, and others who understand their experiences.

Since a large number of the 15-20 percent of the HSP population is to some degree mildly psychic, it is understandable that they are more readily understood by society, with a peer group and resources to back them up, but not by society at large. The percentage of the population that is more sensitive or mildly psychic simply needs some skills and understandings so that their sensitivities do not have physical, mental, and emotional impact on them and to learn how to develop their sensitivities safely and in a correct way.

Sensitivity Checklist

Most people reading this book likely know that they are more sensitive than others and have been told so repeatedly by parents, friends, partners, and others. However, there are basic criteria for knowing that you are part of the 15-20 percent of the population that would be considered as being sensitive. The following traits are found in highly sensitive individuals:

- Easily overwhelmed by to-do lists and tasks.
- Difficulty watching violence, such as in TV and movies.
- Need for separation, alone time, or decompression time, especially after parties and gatherings.
- Difficulty with strong smells, bright lights, loud talking, loud noises.
- Ability to hear, see, feel, and sense more than what presents outwardly in people or places.
- Artistic capabilities, such as writing, painting, music, drawing, acting, or cooking.
- Appreciation of art, ability to use the senses in depth, and noticing of details of artistic expressions.
- Strong imagination and inner life.

Anyone on the spectrum of being considered sensitive will notice these personality traits and inherent talents within themselves. The main criteria for being considered sensitive would be a basic understanding of the self as sensitive, with repeated incidents where one is called "sensitive," "artistic," or "too imaginative," along with a rich inner life and imagination, with occasional feelings of overwhelm when faced with too much stimuli.

People who fit the criteria of being sensitive can be extroverts or introverts and can inhabit a wide range of sensitivity levels. If we consider psychic abilities as simply being sensitive, it would encompass the entirety of this 15-20 percent of the population. Most people who are sensitive would be considered on the end of or early mid-range of sensitivities, meaning that they fit under the criteria above and some of the psychic criteria below but their lives are not impacted to the same extent as those with higher degrees of psychic abilities. In the interest of knowing where you are on the spectrum of psychic abilities, we will discuss generalities between mildly, moderate, and highly psychic capabilities. It is important to note that this is not a contest; it is merely to honestly appraise where you are, and it is not better to be "more" psychic.

It is difficult in some ways to make generalities without considering each person as a unique individual, since psychic abilities can be categorized and present in so many different ways. Understanding where you are on this spectrum will allow you to understand which tools you need and how to move forward. For example, in a mildly psychic state you may be more interested in learning about the spirit world and gaining abilities or noticing even more that surrounds you. In a moderately or highly psychic state, you may need to focus on developing skills and coping mechanisms to deal with your sensitivities, the spirit world, and learning how to function on a day-to-day basis with psychic abilities.

Mildly Psychic

Being mildly psychic means that you fit the criteria for being sensitive and for "highly sensitive people" in the previous section. You will also experience some or all of the following:

- Have an interest in spirituality, in the occult, or in other spiritual matters.
- Are able to read people easily and can tell what they are really like, even if they are lying or presenting differently.
- Can walk into a room and feel if something feels off or not right.
- Feel better emotionally and physically after taking a shower or bath.
- Have moments of inspiration through art, writing, or other forms of expression.
- May have had experiences of mild otherworldly phenomena, such as seeing lights, orbs, and other experiences.
- See the world differently or think differently from others.
- Have difficulty with medications and experience mild illnesses that others cannot explain.
- Have emotions that go up and down for no reason.

Being mildly psychic means that you notice more than those around you. Not only are you sensitive to sounds, smells, emotions, and other sensory information but you are often able to sense hidden emotions and intuitively know information about people, places, and even objects in the room. Being mildly psychic may result in sensitivity to noise, taste, smell, tactile, and visual stimuli. Rather than hearing, smelling, sensing, or otherwise in an extra-sensory manner, meaning that you would sense things in the environment that others cannot, this psychic state allows for heightened senses. This means that you may find yourself hearing from farther away and noises may bother you more than someone in the normal range of perception, or even the highly sensitive range.

For example, consider two people listening to a pop song on the radio, one person has the normal range of perception and one is mildly psychic. The person with the normal range of perception hears the song and either enjoys or dislikes it based on their personal musical tastes. The mildly psychic person, however, may have difficulty with or notice the repetitive nature of the chorus, the bass, and the singer's range. They may also notice the lyrics and the song's meaning, register which song is playing from farther away, or be irritated by the volume of the song.

In the same example as above, the mildly psychic person may be more open to synchronicities or individualized meanings of something such as songs. For example, they may be more likely to attribute a specific song to having a deep meaning in their lives and notice it playing at the perfect time for them personally, or may feel as if songs have messages for them during important periods of their lives. The same holds true for paintings, television shows, conversations, magazines, books, online sources and groups, what time it is on the clock, and other forms of communication and artistic endeavor. The mildly psychic may notice that specific art forms, words, or conversations come to them at the right period or moment in their lives, and they are more likely to pick up when it does.

The same phenomenon occurs for the mildly psychic with their relationship to nature. The mildly psychic may notice that they can communicate on a very basic level with animals and plants and feel as if messages are being given them through the natural world. Communication in this case can be as simple as empathizing with a pet on a deeper level than most pet owners would, to having natural gardening abilities or what is known as a green thumb. Many in the mildly psychic category become interested in nature, symbology of animals and what that might mean for their lives, and feel a pull toward the natural world, such as hiking, camping, or exploring.

There is a tendency in the mildly psychic to over-spiritualize, meaning that they may believe that every animal encounter they have or every song on the radio has a special and significant message for them, or that any time that the clock reads a certain number that it holds specific meaning just for them. There is also a tendency in the mildly psychic to be a seeker of anything that is not readily seen, heard, or felt by normal perception.

In the mildly psychic state, there is often an active interest in learning about energy, spirituality, the occult, religious practices, meditation, and the supernatural. Since you can see and feel more than others, you are interested in knowing more about what cannot be seen, felt, heard, and sensed by most people.

The mildly psychic love to feel in community with others who share their abilities and will often seek out experiences and groups that can foster their sense of having a unique view and understanding of the universe. Through workshops, books, television, and communities of their peers they wish to know more about their experiences and seek out further experiences and understandings of what is going on in their lives. There is an active interest in more exploring and further opening of psychic abilities, and they often seek out others to commiserate about their sensitivity level.

Often, the mildly psychic have experienced supernatural, occult, or energetic phenomena to some degree. They may notice that they naturally are good at reading tarot cards, or that they pick up the basics of essential oils very easily. The mildly psychic are more likely to have experienced or be very interested in seeing ghosts, orbs, angels, energies, UFOs, and other phenomena. There is a natural tendency to not only see but to seek out psychic and even paranormal things, such as visiting haunted hotels, taking psychic classes, watching psychics on television, going to conventions specific to things like energy work, UFOs, psychic phenomena, and enhancing psychic skills. Many in this mildly psychic group join communities, chat rooms, and make friendships based on these mutual experiences and mutual explorations.

Those who are mildly psychic may experience some trauma as a result of feeling more sensitive or different from the general population that is not mildly psychic, but the psychic abilities that manifest in this group are not strong enough to interfere with daily functioning. Frequently those who are in this group will be, as an adult, proud of being considered psychic or sensitive, and will have no issues telling others that they are clairvoyant, psychic, or sensitive, and will lead fairly normal lives.

Others in this group, due to cultural conditioning or religious path, will deny their mildly psychic state or will never consider themselves to be psychic, with few repercussions. They will simply use their intuitive skills in their chosen profession or in the way they live their lives. They may never consider the possibility that their ability to pick up more details in a room and know when someone is lying to them or who to keep away from on the bus may be considered psychic.

The specific physical or emotional complaints that affect people in the moderate to highly psychic abilities group may never be an issue for people who are mildly psychic. Mild digestive upsets, headaches, heart palpitations, or other health complaints may signal overstimulation and the need for decompression or alone time. Those who are mildly psychic may notice that they are more sensitive to hormonal fluctuations and changes in their physical body, such as the menstrual cycle, causing them pain or depression without understanding the cause. Like all psychics, they may become overstimulated and need specific tools to address this, such as visiting healers, learning how to process energy properly, a spiritual hygiene routine, and learning to work with their abilities so that they do not develop physical ailments.

It is common for mildly psychic people to notice that their psychic abilities ebb and flow with the phases of the moon, their stress level, the weather, menstrual cycles, astrological cycles, and what is going on in their personal lives.

This is a natural occurrence for all psychics, not just mildly psychic individuals. However, mild physical symptoms may become more severe in sensitives due to conditions out of their control, such as the weather combined with personal stress and increased sensitivities. Specific tools can keep most of these tendencies under control and improve functioning in the mildly psychic, as well as decrease the physical pain level during increased times of stress, heightened levels of sensitivity, and other global or cosmic occurrences that are making an impact.

It is typical for the mildly psychic to have difficulty containing or expressing their emotions. Sensitivity and expression of emotions are often looked at as a source of weakness or inappropriate, and children still hear the old adage that they should be "seen and not heard," that they are too sensitive, and what they are feeling is inappropriate. Our culture is asleep and does not like to feel or express negative emotions, such as grief, anger, rage, sadness, or depression. If these emotions are expressed, then they are quickly shut down with medications, alcohol and drugs, television, and other numbing behaviors. Even when people have cause to express and deeply feel emotions, such as feelings associated with the death of a family member, other family members, friends, and family may not know how to or want to support the expression of emotions.

This is especially true for psychics. As we notice more, we also feel more. In the mildly psychic category, this can mean that we feel more of our own emotions or that we feel the emotions of other people, places, and even objects in a room. As sensitives, we are more likely to be wounded by the words of others who are in the normal range of sensitivity, and be told when we express hurt that we are being too sensitive.

As discussed later in the book, sensitives and psychics are more likely to pick up the underlying emotions in others and take them on. For example, someone with whom we are conversing in a superficial but pleasant way may have a simmering stockpile of anger from early childhood below the surface that we become aware of. If we are unskilled, we will tend to think that the person is angry with us or about the subject we are discussing, and we are likely to become more stressed out or more emotional than others in the same situation who are not sensitive.

Mildly psychic people may find that they experience a wide range of emotions and are frequently unaware that these may not be their own emotions. They may not have the skill set or understandings to know why they experience a roller coaster of emotions on a regular basis or feel an intense amount of grief when walking into a house when they were happy a few moments ago.

Although most of us realize that we are sensitive, we may not understand that this means that we are frequently reacting to the stimuli we encounter. Experiences of anxiety, fear, or feelings of constantly being "on" are all hallmarks of a nervous system that is constantly triggered. Symptoms such as insomnia, sleeping longer but waking up less rested, and feeling unable to simply "be" rather than "do" are frequently experienced by mildly psychic individuals.

These symptoms are of course dependent on the level of sensitivity and stress level of the mildly psychic, and can be accompanied by such experiences as clinical depression and other mental illness. It is relatively common for the mildly psychic to go through periods of normalcy and then begin to experience stress and heightened stimuli that trigger the nervous system, leading to greater sensitivity levels and issues with sleep. This results in changeable moods and emotions, depending on personal stressors and emotional states, along with sensitivity levels and an inability to understand and process outside emotional stimuli.

Most of the schools that profess to certify mediums, clairvoyants, and other psychics are geared toward helping non-psychic, sensitive, or mildly psychic people become slightly more psychic. Reiki, shamanic journeying, and meditation workshops help the mildly psychic person temporarily or permanently become more open to stimuli in their environment. Without a daily practice such as meditation, the mildly psychic individual is unlikely to become moderately or highly psychic. They may become more sensitive to their surroundings but will likely remain within the range of mildly psychic individuals, despite their efforts.

In some instances, mildly psychic people will experience an event, an opening, or develop a daily practice such as meditation over many years that will allow them to become moderately or highly psychic. They may have a near-death experience (NDE), a sudden revelation of a spiritual nature, an event such as a death in the family, or a sudden realization or remembering of childhood psychic states that propels them into a moderately or even highly psychic state. Having said that, it is rare for anyone to switch from one category of psychic perception to another. Daily or weekly variations may put us at either end of the range, but we may just move from being as sensitive as 18 percent of the population to a higher range of perception, such as found in 12 percent of the population.

As noted earlier, some of us who were highly or moderately psychic as children may have turned off this ability because it is not considered normal or appropriate and created difficulties in school, in our families, or in our communities. Most of us who are moderately or highly psychic do not want to be as psychic as we are—at least initially—and have difficulty accepting our psychic and sensitive natures. Seeing the world differently, or simply seeing, feeling, and experiencing so much, is difficult in a world that mostly fits into the normal range of perceptions. But some of this psychic ability—at a milder, more culturally appropriate level—may have remained with us. When we begin exploring our spirituality, meditating, receiving healing, or just feel ready, we may remember these childhood states of being, allowing psychic abilities to come forward, if we are not blocking them consciously or subconsciously.

Moderately Psychic

Being a moderately psychic person means that you identify with the criteria for highly sensitive and mildly psychic individuals as well as with the following:

- Strange, sometimes intense dreams.
- Feelings of being out of place or out of time.
- A feeling of others, or other energies, that surround you.
- An understanding of spiritual matters without much effort, such as the ability to read tarot cards or a deep love for church.
- Contact with spirit guides, spirits, animal guides.
- A depth to your conversations with other people and dislike for surface level conversations.
- A strong pull or draw to religious or spiritual activities.
- Reaction to weather patterns, such as rain and moon cycles.
- Dietary issues such as inability to process or eat meat, gluten, or sugar.
- A strong reaction to and difficulty with local and world events that you are not connected to, such as school shootings and wars.
- A strong desire to be a seeker and know the spiritual reasons for things, such as diseases, events, or other smaller happenings.
- Health difficulties that are not able to be pinpointed by modern allopathic medicine, diagnosis of a "functional" disease, autoimmune or other conditions such as chronic fatigue or chronic digestive issues.
- Migraines and headaches.
- Heart issues.
- Problems with dizziness or the senses (such as eye and ear issues).
- Mild synesthesia, or the pairing and mixing of stimuli and psychic abilities.

Most people in the mild psychic category are typically fairly functional as long as they get some rest and alone time and other basic self-care measures, such as energetic hygiene. In the moderately psychic state, it is difficult to remain functional without learning appropriate tools and understandings to keep ourselves safe and non-reactionary.

The moderately psychic person may have trouble fitting into normal society. A heightened sense of perception and knowing are typically evident from an early age, and social issues present in early childhood and ado-lescence. Even if moderate psychic abilities emerge out of milder psychic abilities, or when they are older, moderately psychic individuals may find it hard to navigate a world in which 95 percent or so of the population is not as sensitive as they are.

Those of us with moderately psychic abilities may struggle to find peers. Unlike the highly sensitive and mildly psychic individuals, there is such a heightened sense of perception and knowing in the moderately psychic that there are often social difficulties and hardships in living in a world in which you can see and sense so far beyond what other people can. A great deal of emotional trauma and a long path of self-realization often precede our understanding and acceptance of our moderately psychic abilities. We may have a long history of illness and inappropriate care by medical profes-sionals, schools, and our peers, as well as a lack of understanding of what typically defines the path of those with moderate psychic abilities. This will remain true until we learn the skills we need to view our sensitivities as a source of strength rather than a detriment to our lives.

The moderate psychic not only fits into the criteria of mild psychic abili-ties, such as being sensitive to noises or hearing from longer distances, but is able to hear things that others cannot. This may be the thoughts of the people with whom they are engaged in conversation, the thoughts of others in the room, or spiritual sounds such as bells, choirs, or other noises. Mild and moderate psychics typically have a dominant sense: visual, auditory, empathic, felt sense, or kinesthetic sensitivity, or an inner sense of knowing. They may also be able to distinguish different states of the sense, such as people who have a highly psychic sense of taste and are able to tell the dif-ferent notes of wine or a perfumer who is able to distinguish different scents in a perfume.

In the moderately psychic person, there will be more evidence of syn-esthesia, of more than one ability engaging at the same time. An example of this is seeing colors as a result of hearing sound. In its most common expression, someone who has an inner sense of knowing as their dominant sense (claircognizance) will have their senses create a visual of what they are sensing so that they can understand what they are picking up psychi-cally. Many people get confused by this. Because their brains are creating a visual, they will call it "clairvoyance," when, in fact, it is a sense of knowing that is creating the visual for them. This synesthesia and melding of the senses increases with psychic ability. Highly psychic individuals do not need to categorize their abilities through perception (such as the labels of clair-voyance, empathy, and so forth), because they are receiving information through synesthesia, or are simply more open to multisensory experiences.

Along with perceptions of sensory material in a room or in other people, the moderately psychic person has a different understanding of people and the world than do most others, and they may find this difficult to understand and accept. Our schools, and society at large, are centered around a specific way of thinking and being, and anyone who does not conform, or who thinks differently, is often misunderstood or considered an outlier. The moderately psychic individual can truly see, sense, and process stimuli in a way that very few people do. This allows them to bring great ideas, thoughts, and artistry to this world, but can also cause them to feel separated or isolated from people who have "normal" thoughts and experiences of this world.

Most people, psychic or not, are walking around wearing masks. They lie, pretend to be something they are not, and are wounded on a deep level. People put on masks to cover up their wounds so that they will appear stronger, more capable, or more worthwhile than they really feel inside. The moderately psychic is able to sense, look, feel, or use other senses to understand the inner truth or reality of the people around them. This can be difficult in a crowd of people, such as in a bar, where conversation is sup-posed to be light, or one on one, where people may not know, or may not want you to know, what they keep hidden behind their mask.

The moderately psychic individual is able to see things from an expand-ed perspective and see patterns and the symbolic nature of the world. This involves taking a step back from one's own life (and the feeling of being the protagonist or the most important person in the world) and realizing that there are other people out there, all with valid opinions, ideas, and under-standings of the world; that this is true even if they have different opinions and beliefs from our own. On a pattern level, understanding what is going on (the big picture) rather than focusing on detail is a trait that is evident in moderately psychic individuals.

Along with sensing in some way the inner motivations or truths of other people, the history contained within spaces, buildings, and places in na-ture will all show themselves to the moderately psychic person. This can be positive, such as a place of great joy in nature, but it can also be a place of trapped energy or difficult emotions and experiences, such as murders, wars, grief, anger, natural disasters, and other man-made and natural occur-rences that mark a place.

Psychics in this category will not only pick up that something bad happened and perhaps a dominant emotion (as the mildly psychic person would) but be able to sense the events, people, emotions, timelines, and other information about the place. This will all come through the dominant sense or senses for the psychic. They may see it as if it were a silent movie, may hear noises like crying, may smell burning, or may have an inner sense of knowing about what happened at the spot without any other input.

Along with sensing the past the moderately psychic individual is likely to be able to sense or see spirits. In the mildly psychic category, the psychic may experience spiritual phenomena, such as a feeling of something there or a sense of a presence in the home if it is quite strong. This means they may have experiences in haunted houses or places that other people have, or see, feel, or in some way notice spirits that are in a home or other place that are quite dominant. These spirits are emotional, have a message to deliver, or have other reasoning for coming through so strongly that many people can see or sense them.

The moderately psychic person is able to not only sense strong presences but also sense, see, or hear many spirits, even in places where there may not be blatant spiritual activity. Again, there is variability in which sense is dominant (some people may have more spirits around them because they are naturally mediumistic or psychopomps, who are transporters of spirits) and at which end of the spectrum they are as psychics.

Someone who is moderately psychic and notices the same things that 5 percent of the population does is different from someone who is moderately psychic and notices what only 1-2 percent of the population does. In general, the more psychic we are, the more readily we accept that there is more than the physical, concrete reality we consider to be "normal" and the more we sense that the spiritual worlds are a part of our own, not separate places.

There are spirits all around us, all of the time. The moderately psychic person realizes this on some level and can see, feel, or sense spirits in most places. Most of us who are moderately psychic also naturally draw spirits to us due to our abilities. Simply put, we notice them, and so they notice us.

To understand this, we can use the image of a nightlight. We have our normal everyday reality, which most of us can perceive. We will think of this as daylight. But in reality we have many worlds, many layers compressed on top of one another that would be considered the spiritual realms. We can liken these "worlds" to nighttime. As a psychic, we are a nightlight in this spiritual dark, physical beings who operate not only in the everyday reality but to some level on the "other" side, or spiritual reality, or even on other planes of existence.

How bright of a nightlight we are depends on our psychic ability. If we are mildly psychic, we may be a very small nightlight. If we are moderately or highly psychic, we are a bigger and brighter nightlight, meaning that we both perceive more in terms of psychic abilities and spirits and the spiritual realms notice us more—in general, the brighter nightlight we are, the more open and able we are to perceive and the more others perceive us.

Along with moderate psychic abilities come deep spiritual understandings. This can be like the mildly psychic category, in which there is a heightened noticing or looking for messages or synchronicities that have special meaning. The moderately psychic may also notice some of the patterns and symbols that shape our world. This can also be understandings about the nature of the universe, the human condition, healing, plants, animals, artwork, or many other topics. Whereas mildly psychic individuals seek out material and recite books, teachers, and the messages of others, the realizations of moderately psychic people stem from the self—from meditations and direct experience of being someone in the world with psychic abilities.

One of the major indicators of being moderately psychic is the number of dreams people in this category experience, and their intensity. Although intense dreams can certainly be an indicator of psychological issues in anyone, in the moderately psychic person, the dream quality and sensations associated with the dreams are quite different.

The psychic may find themselves having disquieting dreams about lands, times, or events that have no connection to their inner psyche. They may be like a filmstrip or flashes of images, sounds, and memories that do not stem from their experiences. It is also likely that there will be quest dreams, meaning that there is a specific goal in mind for the dream. The inhabitants of quest dreams may or may not be you or concern you at all.

Dreams are also likely to involve spiritual teachers, healing sessions either given or received, or interactions with energy, spirits, beings, or creatures of all types. This is, of course, generally predicated on how psychic the individual is: the more intense the dreams, the more open or advanced the psychic typically is. Once the psychic is skilled, they will be able to work with their dreams, protect themselves if necessary while they are dreaming, or simply call for a night off from having intense dreams.

Dreams are a primary indicator of moderately psychic people because they represent the night aspect, or other side, of our waking world. We are more open to freely interacting in dreams, and it is more rare that we would block ourselves, or know how to block ourselves, from receiving input, symbols, or other meanings during dreamtime. We are free from our physical bodies and are our true essence; this means that we do not have to concern ourselves with the physical restraints of our physical bodies, and what we think to be true about them. We also do not have the rigid ideas of what is commonly referred to and can be seen as the "real" or agreed-upon world and can be ourselves without wearing a mask.

Simply put, we would have no issue flying, meeting strange beings, or being in 1929 in our dreams, but in our daily waking lives we hold onto concrete reality and what we know to be true about ourselves and the world, so meeting a strange being in "ordinary reality" would be upsetting, if not totally freak us out.

Dreams are also a meeting ground. It is a space where worlds meet, and it is easier for spirits and other energies to get through. As sensitives and psychics, we not only gain access to our subconscious in dreams but also to other energies, dimensions, and worlds. It is typical for the moderately psychic individual to have a great deal of difficulty with their dreams in an unskilled state, either feeling as if they want to constantly sleep and never feeling rested due to "traveling" or being unable to sleep due to disruptive dreams or energies in or around them.

Dietary restrictions may be necessary for many mildly psychic individuals, and this is even more true in moderately psychic individuals, in whom it is common to experience strong reactions to chemicals and be unable to eat meat, sweets, dairy, alcohol, specific grains, nightshades, or specific foods for periods of time. Moderately psychic individuals will also find themselves craving the same, typically dense, grounding foods or sweets for quick energy or to help work through the emotional and physical upheavals that come with being sensitive. Gaining and losing of weight, especially around the midsection, is quite common.

When we digest we not only take in food and drink, we also take in and have to process emotions, air, and other energies. According to Traditional Chinese Medicine and other holistic approaches, the digestive system is supposed to take in everything from our daily stresses to food, air and our environment. Most people, psychic or not, have difficulty with their digestive system from high stress levels, resistance or inability to process old emotions and trauma, lack of exercise, and chemicals in food. Not only must psychics contend with digestive difficulties associated with living in a high-stress world, chemical-laden food, and a sedentary society that has difficulty processing emotions and trauma but they also must process the greater amount of stimuli coming through to them as a result of their abilities. Although psychic abilities are considered energetic and spiritual, we are physical people. Our physical, emotional, and energetic selves are all one and work together. When we are inundated with stimuli, we must digest things the best we can, not only on an energetic and emotional level but also a physical level.

If the body is unable to digest food, emotions, or experiences, either from the self or other stimuli, it begins to get backed up and stops processing. It will then start sending signals for quick energy, such as cravings for sweets and carbohydrates. This is followed by further stagnation in the digestive tract and an inability to process foods, leading to inflammation, digestive disorders, and weight gain around the abdomen. This results in an inability to digest certain foods without consequences, such as complex foods (foods with many ingredients), chemical or non-real food, meats, wheat and grains, dairy, and other foods.

We get energy from the reserves of energy given to us through birth and genetics as well as through the food we eat. When we are unable to process our food and gain new energy, we begin to get fatigued and dip into our reserve energy stores.

This is a vicious circle, because when we begin to feel fatigued we reach for caffeine, sweets, carbs, and other foods to pick ourselves up temporarily. These foods cause further inflammation or irritation to the digestive tract, leading to further depletion of energy. The sympathetic nervous system kicks in at some point and puts us in "fight-or-flight" mode, making it even more difficult to digest. It is our parasympathetic nervous system, the body's rest-and-digest mode, which allows us to digest our food. To access this system, our bodies need down time, rest, and enough good-quality sleep. In addition, once our nervous system gets overloaded our immune system crashes, causing systemic issues that are difficult for allopathic providers to figure out and address.

As you can see this is a vicious cycle for most people, psychic or not. Everyone needs to process the events of their day: their stress, their emotions, and their environments. But the psychic notices more and has to process more stimuli, and adverse effects on the digestive system, ensuing fatigue, and feelings of being constantly "on" are common. Later on, immune system issues such as frequently getting sick also occur. Cleaning up the diet, understanding what foods your body intuitively wants, getting appropriate rest, and most of all learning skills such as spiritual hygiene and how to appropriately process energy are necessary for the moderately psychic individual.

Headaches and migraines are very common for the moderately psychic; in part due to digestive difficulties as a result of eating foods our body can no longer process. Migraines, especially for women, can be hormonal. This means that we are more likely to have migraines in response to the menstrual cycle beginning, premenstrually, right after our cycles, or as our luteinizing hormone (LH) surges mid-cycle. However, many of us will find that we get headaches or migraines during different aspects of the moon cycle, astrological cycles, during world or local events, because of fatigue, or other reasons.

One of the bigger reasons for migraines and headaches for the moderately and highly psychic is overwhelm. It is the attempt of the body on a physical level to process the amount of stimuli and energy that it has encountered and stored up. The headache is the way the body tries to process energy along the meridians, or acupuncture channels, in an attempt to disperse or let go of energy that has accumulated. The migraine allows for the backlogged stimuli to be processed and also forces us into a state of rest so that we can process the most amount of stimuli in a short but painful period of time.

In discussing physical manifestations in the bodies of psychics, it's important to note that the mind, body, and spirit are not separate things. For example, many psychics will blame the moon for their headaches, or a war going on somewhere, or an astrological cycle. While this may be true (and skilled psychics still sometimes get headaches), any headache or migraine points to something unhealed that needs to be taken care of. This means that looking not only at the spiritual reasoning, such as a moon cycle or energy outside, but also being open to taking personal responsibility for our emotional state and stress level. It also may mean going to a holistic doctor or allopathic physician and seeing if your hormonal levels, such as thyroid and vitamin D, are in balance; your vitamin and mineral levels, especially magnesium, are adequate; and that contributing factors such as anemia or other issues are not a factor.

Taking personal responsibility for our health, exercise, our emotions, as well as our energetic and spiritual factors is the only way that symptoms such as headaches or migraines will completely clear up. It is common for the mildly, moderately, or even highly psychic individual to go into states of spiritual bypass, or more simply put, blaming everything that occurs on a spiritual or larger reason. While we may have a headache due to a school shooting, especially if we are unskilled, contributing factors like our own anger, hormones, lack of sleep, and other ordinary basic reasons are likely.

Simply put: if we have taken care of our own stuff—our past traumas, emotions, and other issues and our physical selves through diet and exercise—we will significantly cut down on the amount of headaches or other physical issues we have as psychics. More than that, when we learn appropriate skills and boundaries, the spiritual reasons for our headaches are more than likely to disappear altogether. By taking responsibility for not only the spiritual but also our own emotions and experiences in our body we can significantly cut down, or stop altogether, the difficulties that ensue from being sensitive or psychic.

Growing up, many moderately psychic individuals have a long history of counseling, medication, hospitalization, or at the very least many calls from school as a result of being different, and as adults, they may be uncertain about or wish to deny their gifts, seeing it as too much responsibility, too big of a load to carry.

Unlike mildly psychic adults, who are frequently excited about their gifts and willing to share them with the world (or at least find a circle of friends with whom they can complain about their sensitivity levels and how the world affects them), moderately psychic adults are more reticent to speak about their sensitivities. They typically have a long history of not wanting people to find out who they are or what they can do. The moderately psychic frequently have histories of depression and dislike, even hatred, with regard to their abilities, and look at them as a curse, especially if they are unskilled and have not learned how to integrate them into everyday life. Typically, while most mildly psychic people want to learn more and enhance their gifts, most moderately psychic individuals wish to get rid of their gifts, at least at first.

This sentiment can change as the moderately psychic person learns skills to work with their abilities and process the trauma they have endured as a result of them. They understand that their gifts separate them from most of the population in certain ways, but with skill and understanding, they can learn how to construct their lives in order to survive and thrive as psychics, as well as participate in everyday reality. In time, many skilled moderate and highly sensitive psychics see their abilities as a blessing, one that uniquely shows them their place in the world and what they are intended to accomplish here.

Relationships and friendships can be difficult for the moderately psychic, due to their ability to tune into the inner workings of people and places. The moderately psychic are able to see more deeply into a topic or view topics differently from most people. Simply put, they are on another wavelength than most of society. The moderately psychic person has a need to find the inner truth of people and situations and has a uniquely multifaceted view of the world. They display critical thinking that much of the population has lost. The more psychic we become, the more we are able to have multiple layers of understanding and move away from superficiality, as well as beliefs simply because they were taught us by others.

This ability to see, feel, hear, or sense things differently from others creates negative experiences and trauma in the life of the psychic but also a capacity for artistic expression, depth of thought, and unique ways of thinking that can allow the psychic to bring their gifts to the world through a variety of media. Artwork such as painting or drawing, acting, cooking, writing, and studying allow them outer expression of their inner world and depth. Many of the world's great artists, visionaries, and luminaries are moderately psychic and have given the world new inventions, works of art, plays and movies, written works, perfumes, and foods that are extraordinary.

Most of the world operates at a very surface level of understanding and considers things to be black or white, either/or, and this will persist in the mildly psychic group: they will find exact definitions for healing methods, look up the meanings of animals they encounter in dictionaries, and view spiritual happenings around them as having a specific meaning or answer. For them, the search for meaning will be defined by outside sources, such as a guru, teacher, or friend who tells them what to think and how to define their experiences.

The more psychic an individual, the more likely they are to acknowledge what they do not know, that there is no one answer, or even an answer at all, to many questions. They are open to learning from all sources and demonstrate a constant deepening to experiences, understandings, and cosmology. Their understandings are also more likely to come from direct experience, or inner realization, than through outer sources such as teachers, books, and workshops.

Most spiritual communities are comprised of the mildly psychic, the aspirational psychic, or the non-psychic, who will not be able to understand the experiences or be able to connect with the knowledge of the moderately or highly psychic. There is, in fact, a state of cognitive dissonance in place that will not allow for the mildly or non-psychic to understand people who have experiences so far out of their direct experience or comfort zone. Although the ability to see and know things that relatively few people do allows for great insight and works of artistry, as well as a rich inner life, it is difficult for the moderately psychic individual to find others that will understand them or connect with them, or a community to be a part of.

It is no surprise that many of the psychic entertainers on television, the self-appointed gurus in groups, and the resources out there are intended for those who are aspirational, sensitive, or mildly psychic. This is unfortunately how and why there is so much false or silly information out there. Much of it is coming from individuals who are promising the world that they can become "Psychic in Six Easy Steps!" but lack any sort of abilities or self-cultivation themselves. In many cases, it is much easier to be a guru or teacher than to cultivate the self. These people populate our chat rooms, our television sets, and are our friends and communities. Moderately psychic individuals know that there is no teaching, no routine, no teacher who will have us go from step one to step five for $99.95.

Since we live in a society that is unable to look beyond the superficial, and wants to be advanced or highly psychic in a few simple steps, moderately psychic individuals frequently have anger, grief, or issues relating to spiritual and psychic communities. They realize that most people are beginners, and want to remain beginners. They feel angry, knowing that most people who are loudly shouting that they are clairvoyant would run screaming in the other direction if they actually saw anything or experienced anything of a spiritual nature directly.

Even the most advanced, skilled, and accepting psychics must contend with the fact that the majority of information about psychic abilities, spiritual paths, or simply information in the news and from other sources contains many falsehoods. Eventually, most psychics can develop compassion for even fake or aspirational psychics, and some may even be willing to teach them. Many may choose to remove themselves from communities and groups that they do not relate to. In time, with the support of a few teachers or guides, they will be able to embrace being outliers, and use this capability to bring new ideas, thoughts, and understandings to the world that can benefit humanity as a whole. Such people, if they allow their abilities to open and become skilled, will follow and be guided to a deeply spiritual path.

Many belief systems, rules, and guidelines are taught in spiritual communities. These can be as simple as which color is associated with which chakra to which hand receives healing during energy work. Although definitions, teachings, and teachers can be helpful for any type of psychic, the moderately psychic will need to forge their own path and will require inner teachings and spiritual non-physical teachers to develop what their own truth is.

Many of the rules and paradigms are created to teach non-psychic and mildly psychic people and to keep them confined in a certain way to specific teachings, and to feel safe and in control of their spiritual experiences. The moderately psychic will have direct experience of things that go against the established rules or teachings, or may not be discussed or known at all by teachers or through books. Many of the deeper teachings of the world and the universe are not taught in books—they must be directly experienced. They are too hard to put into words, and nobody would believe them anyhow. Most books and teachers are for the majority, the non-psychic and mildly psychic, which comprises about 95 percent of the population.

At some point, or at several points, the moderately psychic person will have the opportunity to have direct experiences of spirituality and their individual spiritual path. At first, they typically try to fit their experiences into the box that has already been formed by so many others to confine and define us. When they do not find their experiences in books, or find a vague semblance of them online or in chat rooms, they will try to fit their experiences into others that are more concrete or seem more established. Even worse, they will ask online and get advice from mildly or non-psychic individuals who seek to define their experiences for them and who have little idea what they are talking about and are just regurgitating questionable material from books or other resources.

Although it is difficult to understand, most moderately psychic individuals will have to either find a highly psychic individual or a more psychic individual than they are (perhaps still in the moderate category) to discuss their experience with, if they do at all. Highly psychic and moderately psychic individuals who are skilled or advanced will know that spiritual and psychic experiences do not fit an easy dictionary definition and cannot be contained within arbitrary rules. In fact, defining or explaining away experiences can be harmful, as the psychic is likely to not notice an important message or part of the experience as it relates to their personal filter, or their prior experiences and understandings of this world.

Later in this book, we will discuss creating a personal library, or internal filing system, to understand our own spiritual experiences. But one of the greatest examples of how outer culture defines and restricts psychic abilities is the following example.

Three people with mild to moderate psychic abilities may have an influx of spiders in their home. All three ask online what this means. They are all given the definition that spiders mean creativity, that spider medicine is strong, and that spiders are a good helper to have.

In reality, one of these people simply lives in a place where the weather is cold and spiders are coming in. It has no real spiritual meaning. If anything, it means she needs an exterminator or to remove spiders through natural means from her house. The second had a childhood incident of watching her brother pull the legs off daddy long-legs and placing them on her shins to watch them squirm. She can still remember the sensation and has been deeply afraid of spiders ever since. The spiders in her case are showing her that her fears are coming out of the woodwork, so to speak. She should work on the emerging fears that are coming up to clear the spiders. The third person is a man who frequently sees spiders and has a sense of understanding or knowing with them. In exploring this further, he was able to see that spiders show up when he connects with his ancestry.

In this example, we can see how the typical, or dictionary-defined definition, is given for all three cases. All three of these psychics are individuals, with individual histories as spiritual abilities. If they were to listen to the group, or the held conventions of thinking that the spider means creativity, rather than listen to their own inner guidance about what was going on they would have missed a very important lesson or message. By developing relationships, tools, and understandings as moderately psychic individuals we can uniquely assess and know what is going on in our spiritual relationships, through the lens of our own experiences in this world and our own filter. In this way, we can also demonstrate common sense. We can see the world as a place where spiders may have a message and may be a great spiritual occurrence for us, or they simply call our attention to the fact that our basement needs an exterminator and a contractor to fix some leaks.

It is important for the moderately psychic person to develop relationships with non-physical teachers and develop their inner intuition and guidance system to help them navigate their experiences. Although it is important to have physical teachers as a catalyst, or to teach you the skills necessary to develop inner guidance, spiritual power, and non-physical teachers, the appropriate teacher for the moderately psychic people (or really anyone) will teach us how to find the answers for ourselves. The universe, and especially the spiritual realms, are not neatly divided, easily explained, black-or-white places. The appropriate physical, living breathing teacher will know this.

If the moderately psychic individual chooses to define themselves by the experiences of others because of fear or due to a lack of skill, they will either constrict their abilities, causing them to not be as open as they once were, or they will cause them to stagnate, preventing them from opening farther. While many people in this group may have wished at one time that they did not have abilities, or have difficulty with some of the repercussions of being so sensitive, when they accept and learn how to open their abilities they can work with them and make their lives easier.

The more skill and knowledge the psychic has, the less they will have issues with their abilities, and the more benefit their sensitivities will bring to their life. The less drama, stress, chaos, past trauma, and physical issues present in the body of the psychic, the easier it is to handle having even the strongest psychic abilities. It is natural for the moderately psychic individual to at first constrict, deny, or obstruct their abilities, either consciously or through belief systems. These obstructions cause physical, mental, emotional, and spiritual issues. When we learn appropriate skills and tools for working with our abilities, we can be fully protected, safe, and more open to experiencing them as a gift, rather than as a detrimental force in our lives.

In many cases, the moderately psychic person will at first confine their experiences to what they have read and what their community or appointed guru or teacher tells them. This may happen even if the moderately psychic individual realizes that the people online, the self-appointed guru, or the book that they are reading is coming from someone of lower psychic awareness than them. When the moderately psychic confine their experiences to the understandings of these people, they will eventually change their experiences and memories of the experience to fit in with what people have told them about the experience. This causes a constriction of their abilities, and may even result in physical repercussions for the psychic. They have been given an opportunity to trust their inner guidance, their intuition, and their psychic senses, but have instead opted to remain safe and in the known. By staying with the known, and letting the experiences and knowledge of others define their own experiences, they may have lost an important part of the message, experience, or even a spiritual type of initiation to further open their abilities or learn something interesting about themselves and the world.

In addition to relying on the experiences and teachings of others to define our experiences, the other way that moderately psychic individuals restrict themselves by is ego. A healthy, functional, self-defined sense of self and confidence in that self, or ego, is crucial to our stability—mentally, emotionally, physically, and spiritually. However, if we start to think that we are at the end of our journey, that we are better or more psychic than others, that we have all the answers, or that we know all of the answers in the universe, we restrict ourselves and remain where we are. This is true for everyone—mildly, moderately, and highly psychic individuals, as well as non-psychics.

But when we believe ourselves to know everything, there is no reason to know more. When we appoint ourselves as gurus, teachers, and guides, simply the act of doing so can stop our growth and create blockage in our abilities. It is easy to lose clarity when we come from a place of ego. It is easy to create a world of illusion in which we have all the answers and have followers, or students, or friends who constantly ask us for advice. It is very easy to fall into the trap of having everything be one-sided. We are the guru, the psychic, the teacher. We know everything and teach other mildly or moderately psychic people to come up to our level.

At its best, the teacher-student relationship is beautiful, but if the teacher is coming from a place of ego all too often it creates a lack of clarity and leads to stagnation in their abilities. The teacher is no longer open to being wrong, no longer can ask for help on their own path, and no longer makes progress.

When the moderately psychic person opens themselves up to the fact that they cannot possibly know everything, and that no matter how psychically able they are, there is always someone out there who sees, feels, or senses more than they do, or can sense things differently, then they can move out of a place of stagnation. When they open up about their own issues in an appropriate way, this can show their followers, students, and clients the truth of who they are. When they are open to constantly knowing more, experiencing more, and exploring their abilities in a skilled way, the pain, isolation, and difficulties they experience will lessen considerably.

The moderately psychic may also be consciously or subconsciously closing down their abilities. We will discuss this further later on, but in general, this is due to a fear of being overwhelmed or an uncertainty or lack of control on the part of the psychic. While they can learn skills to control and work with their abilities, they must come to realize that they only have a certain degree of control and must learn to surrender. They can learn appropriate tools, boundaries, clearing and cleansing techniques, as well as energetic techniques and meditations, to help process the stimuli coming in. But being moderately psychic is not a choice made by the individual; it is something that they experience and is their inherent way of being in the world. The moderately psychic individual falters because they rarely understand which tools they need to modulate, or work with, their abilities.

Since there is so little information out there for people with this level of psychic ability, they must move through a great deal of fear, as well as reconcile feelings of being "different." Most spiritual communities make an effort to have "safe practices" to keep the aspirational shaman, spiritual worker or psychic safe—safety nets, so to speak. Most of us immersed in the spiritual realms, and that which is hidden but in plain sight, do not have a safety net. Feelings of fear come up as a byproduct of feeling out of control or victimized by the circumstances that emerge.

It is easy to be safe in the mildly psychic or non-psychic categories, as in most cases, our spiritual helpers, spiritual understandings, and practices are either created by us or represent a disassociated aspect of ourselves. In moderately psychic states, however, it is common to have spiritual issues, initiations, and other happenings that are so out of our control that we are deeply afraid. We are unable to discuss these happenings with others, because we know that they are out of line with what most people feel, see, and understand. The more psychic we are, the more we are likely to have direct experiences of a spiritual nature, ones that do not easily fit a mold or a safety net.

Moderately psychic people are often highly spiritual people. We can hear the call to a specific path, identify with various religions or spiritual prac- tices quite readily, and are able to see, sense, hear, and feel things stemming from the spiritual realms. Although this is not a book on spiritual awaken- ings, psychic abilities are considered a byproduct of being awakened, or awakening, and an ability to see, feel, hear, and sense more is a natural prod- uct of spiritual unfolding and greater awakening. As highly spiritual sorts, we find peace and beauty in simple things, are often non-materialistic, and are able to tell if we are going down the right path or not in our lives. We often feel a pull to be of service in a specific way, often utilizing our abilities. We may have the ability to communicate deeply not only with other people but with plants, animals, and the universe itself.

Moderately psychic people will feel the need to decompress often to remain physically and mentally healthy. Disappearing into nature, meditation, yoga, alone time, and other mind/body pursuits are necessary to be able to function. The ability to understand and in some way communicate with others will allow them to take up gardening and have relationships with animals, plants, flowers, and tree life, depending on interests.

Moderately psychic people may recall past lives and have an awareness of ancestral issues, or karma. They may be slightly aware of the grids and energies that make up the universe. They may also have preliminary understandings or encounters with beings other than spirits, such as elementals, extraterrestrials, deities, as well as other dimensions and galaxies. Much of this takes place with highly psychic individuals, but the moderately psychic, especially those higher on the spectrum, will have an awareness, understanding, or have direct experience of some of these.

It is typical for moderately psychic people to not accept their stranger experiences or not talk about them with others for fear of what others may think or say about them. Since such experiences are so far out of the possibility of the normal range of perception, there is also understandably a fear of being thought mad, being medicated, or at the very least lacking the confidence or words to even describe stranger and more powerful experiences that occur in the higher psychic states.

Many of the higher moderately psychic states are overwhelming to the unskilled individuals experiencing them, and so out of the realm of possibility for non-psychics as well as mild and moderate psychics that they are simply not discussed. As psychic abilities heighten, there is an associated decrease in the person's ability to remain functional in the day-to-day world, and even such simple activities as a quick trip to the grocery store may prove difficult for those with heightened psychic senses as long as they remain unskilled.

Typically, the more heightened the abilities, the more dysfunctional the psychic, until they are able to get the appropriate tools and understandings to work with their gifts. And even then, the amount of stimuli during specific times may prove just too much for those in the higher moderately psychic state.

Highly Psychic

A highly psychic state is fairly rare and means that you fit into the moderately psychic, mildly psychic, as well as the sensitive categories and also experience the following:

- Intense dreams and dream states that are not "of you"—meaning they are of people, places, and events in no way connected to you.
- Family members or ancestors who were psychic.
- Incidents of death or near-death.
- Moderate to severe childhood trauma.
- A feeling of traveling either in dreams or during the day to help others or a feeling of simply being somewhere else energetically or spiritually.
- Daily incidents and happenings of a spiritual nature.
- Constant synchronicities.
- Seeing, feeling, or sensing full-body apparitions such as spirits on a daily basis.
- Seeing, feeling, or sensing the grid system or communal energies that make up our society and world.
- Continual processing, i.e., releasing of events of your life, your birth, immediate family, past lives, and so forth.
- Understanding, feeling, or seeing your past lives and how they affect you.
- Connection to ancestors and ancestry.
- Ability to feel land and earth energies, such as vibrations.
- Ability to view or understand karmic patterns.
- Ability to see and feel patterns, loops, and grids that comprise the universe.
- Healing abilities or other powers.
- Processing not only of events connected to you and your family but a processing of events in the world through you.
- Non-physical spiritual teachers and guides that are not of you or created by you.
- Ability to travel through spiritual gateways.
- Experience spirit-led initiations.
- Have deep understandings of a spiritual nature about the world.
- Difficulty accepting psychic abilities.
- Severe medical issues without cause.
- Decrease in functioning in daily, regular life due to abilities (unless a suitable teacher has been found).

In the highly psychic states, there is typically no longer a differentiation be-tween "types" of psychic abilities, such as clairvoyance or clairaudience. The psychic who fits into the highly psychic criteria will have merged all of their abilities. Although the highly psychic may still have a dominant ability, such as clairvoyance, they will typically have a multisensory experience of psychic phenomena. They may see something in front of them as if it were a short film, complete with sound, lighting, and emotional and visual experiences, or experience synesthesia, where an ability triggers another or is experienced through another pathway (such as sound creating a visual).

The highly psychic person often does not have a choice about their path. They are so in touch with what surrounds them, and are so sensitive to it, they cannot go back to sleep and prevent themselves from seeing, feeling, touching, or working with things on a deep level.

Unskilled psychics who fall into this category have a fair number of medical, emotional, and spiritual imbalances, and unless they get the right tools and teacher and learn how to work with their gifts, they are likely to have difficulty functioning in their daily lives. Even if the highly psychic individual does have the appropriate skills to navigate their psychic experiences, they will require time alone to decompress from them. The highly psychic individual may need to live in a space that allows them a fair amount of personal space, and will often have difficulty with apartments or highly populated areas due to their sensitivity level.

The highly psychic person is likely to suffer from a variety of medical issues, especially autoimmune, fatigue, and emotional imbalances due to their constant immersion in overwhelming stimuli and the wide variety of spiritual states and spiritual material that they come into contact with. Even skilled highly psychic individuals have difficulty maintaining boundaries and working without becoming ill. They must learn tools and consistently work with them in order to have a functional and healthy way of life.

As noted earlier, it is very typical that the more psychic someone is the more difficulty they have accepting it, although in rare cases someone will come from a family that has several skilled psychic members who can help a child or young adult accept and learn how to work with their abilities. Generally, the more skills and knowledge the highly psychic individual has, the more they will accept their abilities and consider them a gift rather than a curse.

This means that we can release some or all of the stigma of feeling different from others, the feeling that our abilities are a curse, and the various traumas and other emotional issues that have arisen living life as a highly psychic individual in a world that is not.

Even with the full skill set and understandings of being highly psychic, it is rare for the highly psychic person to be excited about their abilities at certain times in their lives—they can be sometimes just too painful and difficult to deal with. But by learning how to work with their gifts, they can come to a state of acceptance, of peace, and of possessing knowledge that very few people in this world have. A state of feeling blessed and of deep knowing can come, as well as the tools and understandings to create a life in which we can thrive. The highly psychic person can step into their ability to see, sense, or feel differently from others and their outlier path in this world as a source of strength.

Those of us who are highly psychic often require careers and relationships that support our abilities and unique view of the world. We typically do best in non-traditional work that has variable hours and affords time off and in relationships in which the partner is understanding of our need for privacy and isolation.

For the highly psychic person, abilities come in waves. Some days may bring such extreme sensitivity that we need to remain in bed all day; on others, we can go about our daily lives in normal or almost normal fashion. These waves will keep happening as long as the highly psychic individual remains unskilled. In time, the highly psychic person may notice a correlation in sensitivity with the menstrual cycle (in females) or other hormonal cycles (in men), diet, astrological occurrences, moon cycles, and world events. Highly skilled highly sensitive psychics will be able to understand and prepare for days when they will be less functional as well as days when they may be able to get a huge amount done.

One of the biggest distinctions between the highly psychic and more moderate states is the level of processing that occurs. While the mildly or moderately psychic individual may notice planetary events such as Mercury Retrograde or complain about feeling weird around a full moon or emotionally impacted by a bombing or school shooting, the highly psychic person will actually process these events through their bodies. When we are very connected to the spiritual, as we are in highly psychic states, we not only process our own material (our past traumas) but our past lives, ancestral issues, family issues, and community, global, and cosmic issues.

Moderately psychic individuals may be aware that something like a school shooting impacts us and that we feel emotions not only in reaction to it but to the grief of the community where it occurred, or even to the event itself. Highly psychic individuals not only have a personal emotional response but process the actual event, becoming a sort of spout, fault line, or volcano for large and small-scale events that are happening locally and globally. As highly psychic individuals, we become release valves for the built-up emotions and energies that are created by these events.

As highly psychic individuals, we have an understanding of spirits, energies, lands, universes, and worlds beyond this one. Although difficult to describe without directly experiencing it, we are aware that there are many worlds beyond those we consensually call "reality," that time and space are an illusion, and that the spiritual permeates everything we do. We are able to see and sense the grid system, or basically the fabric of our varying realities. We are able to be a strong nightlight that attracts a wide variety of spiritual experiences, understandings, and contact with a large number of spirits and beings.

For severely unskilled highly psychic individuals, this ability to see through realities and make contact with a wide variety of other spirits and beings may bring with it an inability to stay grounded in this world, or to differentiate that this is the consensual, agreed-upon reality that we must outwardly live in. We all should be in our physical reality predominantly, but some people in the highly psychic category tend to drift between worlds without an anchor in this one. This leads to hospitalization, medication, and a wide variety of other issues.

In skilled states, the openness that is provided by being highly psychic can lead to ever deepening understandings and direct experience of spiritual matters that are not frequently discussed in books or would not be understood by most of the population. Individuals who fall into this category—even more so than those in the mildly and moderately psychic categories—can use their unique abilities and understandings to benefit the world in a way that few others can, and have experiences of a spiritual nature on a regular basis that others can only aspire to.

CHAPTER THREE

Working with Psychic Abilities – Basic Skills

Now that we have reviewed in some detail the specific abilities associated with each psychic category, from highly sensitive to mild to moderate to highly psychic, the next step is to identify your own level of ability and determine which category you fall in.

Write out a list of the ways that you feel that you are sensitive; maybe even some defining events in your life that have shown you are psychic. By understanding your psychic ability, you can begin to work with basic psychic tools and gain skills. We will work with the basic skill set that all sensitives and psychics should develop. Remember: when we are able to gain skills, such as understanding and learning how to work with our abilities, we can begin to thrive in our lives.

The purpose of learning how to work with psychic abilities is so that you can have a meaningful, functional life. Unskilled sensitives and psychics simply do not have the tools that they need to learn how to manage their abilities.

The rest of this book provides the skills, or tools, you will need to become a skilled psychic and includes exercises on developing boundaries, understanding who you are, spiritual hygiene, and protection. If practiced diligently, these tools will allow any psychic or sensitive, no matter how their psychic abilities or sensitivities present themselves, to work with their abilities, have a sense of understanding and control, and stop any overwhelm that may be occurring.

As with any tool, these exercises are meant to be done over time, and with patience. This means that we rarely understand something or fully embody it the first time, or even the fiftieth. By working with each tool individually, then adding the next when the first feels quite fluid, you can develop all of these tools strongly and have them be extremely effective for you.

In terms of how to progress with these tools, I suggest working with the basic skills for a few months on a regular basis before proceeding to the intermediate skills. The basic skills are intended to allow you to understand who you are on a deep level, as well as open you up to process stimuli in a more grounded, healthy way. When these skills have been fully developed, the intermediate skills, which focus on understanding our energetic and spiritual natures and developing a skill set to work with spiritual energies, will come more naturally and readily.

When you begin to work with these tools, pick one or two of the basic skills to work with. You may also wish to look ahead to begin doing spiritual hygiene methods (spiritual bathing and house clearing) at the same time. When you develop each skill to the point that it is second nature to you, you can pick another basic skill to learn. Go through the basic skills first before going on to the intermediate skills.

Once you have gone through the basic and intermediate skills, and have a solid cleansing and clearing routine in place, skills such as developing boundaries and protections will make more sense to you and come more readily. As with any skill, looking back at some of the skills, even after you have worked with them for a while, can allow you to gain new insight or a deepening of the practice.

Going forward, the word "psychic" will be used to mean the full spectrum of sensitivities, from highly sensitive to highly psychic, as these are all skills that every sensitive and psychic, no matter where they are on the spectrum, should use. It is true, however, that a mildly psychic person may just need a few of the skills, such as some of the basic skills and a personal hygiene routine, while a moderately or highly psychic individual is more likely to need all of these tools and to learn them over a period of time, such as a year of in-depth study.

No matter where you fall on the spectrum of psychic ability, the focus of all these tools is on what you need to know in order to learn how to manage your psychic abilities. So let's get started.

Is This Mine?

As psychics, we are constantly having to process and notice things in our environment and from other people that do not come from us. This means that we not only have to deal with our own struggles and stimuli—emotions, traumas, to-do lists, jobs, errands, children, school, and what our daily lives contain—but also stimuli from people around us, the place we are in, even objects, communal events, world events, and so forth. This is understandably overwhelming, and all psychics need to learn to deal with it.

Our minds and bodies do not have a natural filing system for information and stimuli coming at us that is not ours. This means that if we do not have this skill, which will be taught below, our bodies naturally assume that all stimuli coming at us and into us is our own, and we need to process it and "digest" it much like we do our own emotions and what we eat. In fact, we do not need to do this. If we learn how to create this "filing system," we can train ourselves to understand what is ours and process it, and what is not ours and effectively simply let that go.

No matter how large the stimuli—whether it is coming from the weather outside, the cosmos, or the anger from the guy sitting across from you on the train—you can learn how to filter and process this information. All it requires really is one simple question, as well as a baseline understanding of who you are (which we will learn in the next section).

This is a deceptively simple question. When we identify as psychic or sensitive, we know that we have to deal with stimuli that is very much ours. We can take responsibility for it; for example, if we eat pizza and a cupcake at lunch, we may not feel well in the afternoon. However, we also have to deal with a huge range of stimuli that is not ours. By beginning to ask the question of "Is this mine?" we can begin the basic process of sorting. Sorting allows us to begin to discard stimuli that is not ours. Once we develop pathways, or channels, to dispose of stimuli, the question of "Is this mine?" allows us to identify and then dispose of most stimuli that is not ours.

EXERCISE: Is This Mine?

> Sit for a moment and simply notice an emotion or physical sensation rise to the surface. Whatever gets your attention is fine. When you notice this, ask "Is this mine?" You will get an answer—either yes, no, or confusion. If you do not get an answer, you can try again later. Do not doubt your intuition. It is frequently the case for many of us that we do not allow ourselves to experience what is the most common psychic sense, claircognizance, or a clear sense of intuitive knowing. Our gut instinct can be listened to and cultivated for clear answers in this exercise, as well as throughout our whole existence. All it requires is for us to listen to and give credence to that little voice inside.
>
> If the answer is "yes," as in, this pain or emotion belongs to us, say "thank you" for the information and simply sit with the pain or emotion for a moment, acknowledging it. When we acknowledge something, we can begin to process or work with it consciously. Of-

ten we tend to disassociate or run away from painful emotions and physical sensations. By sitting with them, even when they are ours, they can feel heard and seen. By allowing our pain to be heard and seen consciously by us, it may be open to leaving or lessening naturally. All pain is a signal, or information, in our body that is trying to tell us something. It may be whispering to us or screaming at us. By acknowledging the pain we are experiencing, we are taking personal responsibility for it and allowing it to become conscious. This will naturally lessen some of the pain response, especially if we do this over time.

If the answer is "no," then you know that this pain or emotion originated from outside of you. By acknowledging this, and that it is not yours, it will lessen or disappear. So if you hear, "No, my hip pain is not mine" or "No, this grief is not coming from me," you can say, "I acknowledge that this is not mine. I ask anything that is not mine to leave," and allow it to go.

You will do this by imagining the pain or emotion as a color. Choose the color that is best for the situation; you do not have to choose the same color every time. Imagine this color and where it lies in your body. With physical pain this may be easier, but with emotions you may have to do a body scan, starting at the feet and going up to the top of the head.

For example, ask for any anger that is not yours to show up in a specific area of your body. When it does, inquire if it is yours. If it is not, imagine it as a color, such as red. Imagine how much red you have in your body, and where it is. When you are ready, you will simply imagine breathing this color out through your mouth or imagine it running down your legs and out the soles of your feet into the earth. Choose whichever route seems easiest. If you are ungrounded and not fully in your body, breathing out a color is typically the easiest thing to do for this exercise.

Continue breathing until you no longer notice the color in your body. This sounds deceptively simple, I realize. But this is one of the most effective tools a sensitive and psychic can have. The more that you can do basic sorting—understanding what is yours and what is not—the easier it is for the body to let go of stimuli that is not yours.

In some cases, the answer you receive may be more vague, or may be a yes-and-no response. In this case, even more sorting is necessary. Ask your body for what is not yours, acknowledge it, and invite it to leave. In many cases, we feel comfortable with percentages. If you are feeling hip pain and get a yes-and-no response to "Is this mine?" you can ask internally, "How much is mine?" You may get a percentage, such as 50 percent. In this case, you would acknowledge the 50 percent that is not yours and invite it to leave by engaging in the same color exercise. You would then feel the remainder—the 50 percent that is yours, acknowledge it, and simply sit with it for a moment.

Although this is a simple skill, it is an essential building block for the rest of the skills and boundaries. Just by asking, "Is this mine?" whenever we feel any sort of stimulus, physically, emotionally, or spiritually, we may be surprised by how our body responds and consciously realize how much of what we carry is, in fact, not ours. As we work with this skill over time, we can expand it and our bodies will have an easier time sorting out what's ours and what's not. In the beginning, things may be fuzzy for us. We may not get a response, or may not get a clear response. In time, just asking the question "Is this mine?" will allow the body to automatically clear anything that is not yours.

Summary

- Notice a pain or emotion in your body. One may be quite evident, or you can choose to do a body scan (start at the feet, go up to the head and down the arms, asking for a body part to highlight that you can work with).
- When you find a body part or emotion located in a body part, bring gentle focus to that area of your body.
- Ask the question: Is this mine?
- You will hear an answer: yes, no, or maybe (or confusion).
- If it is yes, simply acknowledge the pain or emotion, e.g. "Yes, I feel angry. Yes, I have pain in my hip. Yes, I had too many slices of pizza for lunch...."
- If it is no, imagine the pain or emotion as a color. Use whichever color is appropriate for this area of your body this moment.
- Now breathe out this color through your mouth. Picture it leaving your body through your breath when you exhale.
- If it feels more natural, you can imagine this color running down your legs and out of the soles of your feet into the earth.

- Check in and see how much of the color is left. Or maybe it is a new color you can breathe out or let go out of your feet.
- Work with your color until you no longer notice it.

It is common to feel confused, or as though the answer is both yes and no (partially yours and partially not) when you ask the question of "Is this mine?" In that case:

- Ask for the percentage that is yours (20 percent? 50 percent?).
- Acknowledge what is yours, as you did above.
- Imagine what is not yours as a color, and repeat the exercise above.

It is very common for psychic stimuli to become congested in areas of personal weakness and imbalance to us. This means that the hip we injured in soccer practice, the knee from diving into a lake as a small child, or the lung area where we hold the grief from a parent dying are areas of imbalance in us. It is easy for areas in our body that are struggling already with our own "stuff" to take on energies that are not our own.

As discussed in previous sections, it is also quite common for psychic stimuli to get stuck in the digestive tract and the head, due to our need to digest any type of energy coming into us—whether it is ours and a basic resource (such as the food we take in), or our own emotions, or the emotions of the world. We may then get overwhelmed and experience digestive issues, headaches (from our bodies trying to process so much stimuli), heart issues, fatigue, immune imbalances and other physical issues from not having this natural filtering system. The more that we can create this filter for ourselves, the more natural it will become.

For even the speediest learner, the exercise *Is This Mine?* may need to be done over a period of a few weeks many times a day. After a certain point, our body and mind catch on and without prompting begin processing stimuli that are not ours. Even then, we all have "off" days, or days when we are overstimulated, so asking the question "Is this mine?," even when our body is typically processing stimuli without our input, is helpful; in fact, it is essential, even for the most highly skilled psychic.

Basic Discernment

Once we can acknowledge what is not ours, we can learn basic discernment skills to know where specific stimuli has originated from. In time, we can learn to sense and know when different types of stimuli are coming our way, and from where.

To do this, we can first work with the *Is this Mine?* exercise. When we notice something within our body that is not ours, or is partially not ours, instead of exhaling it right away, we can sit with it for a moment and engage in a questioning process. Although there are many different types of stimuli that we can take on, there are some that are more common. You will sit with the color and energy of what is not "yours" and ask it the following questions:

- Are you an emotion? If so, what emotion?
- Are you a thought? If so, what thought?
- Are you a physical issue that I have taken on from someone else?
- Are you a spirit or being?
- Are you a cosmic energy (such as weather, astrological fluxes, moon cycle, and so forth)?
- Are you from an event happening in the world? What event?
- Are you energy from a place or land?

These basic questions will allow you to begin to understand the basic type of stimuli you are dealing with. The purpose in asking these questions (instead of simply getting rid of the stimuli) is to create a more specialized filing system. When we ask the above questions, we are relying on our sense of knowing (claircognizance) to have a sense of which answer is correct. We can ask the above questions to ourselves and just listen for an internal "yes" or "no," which is likely to provide us with a clear answer as to the source of the energy.

Through practice of the above, we may discover that we tend to take on the emotions of others predominantly; or we may notice that we tend to take thoughts or mental energies from other people into our solar plexus. We may even find that when we take on the emotion of anger that it tends to be an orange color, while energies we have absorbed from our office building tend to be blue.

It is possible to take on a wide variety of energies from our environment, places we visit, the thoughts and emotions of other people, as well as even larger happenings, such as earthquakes occurring halfway around the world. It is easy to get caught up in your findings, but the purpose of understanding what sort of stimuli you tend to take on is for the purpose of properly "digesting" it so that it does not create issues for you.

Discernment – Part Two

In further discerning energies we take on, we can understand who we are as psychics, as well as learn to begin to build a "library" of our experiences (how to fully develop this library is detailed later in the "Developing a Psychic Library" section). The more information that we can begin to gather about the sort of stimuli we have taken on the easier it is for us to process, or for us to process similar stimuli in the future.

If we are unable to discern the source of psychic stimuli we experience, we are more likely to fear our abilities. The more we understand about our sensitivities, the more empowered we can become, and the more we can understand who we truly are in this world. Discernment is a key process that every psychic should learn to feel in control of their sensitivities and psychic abilities.

After we ask the questions above, we may be ready for further discernment. Once we have determined that an energy is not ours, and have basically figured out the source, we can move on to the following questions:

- How long ago has this energy been present?
- Where did I pick up this energy?
- Who did I pick up this energy from?
- Why was this energy attracted to me?
- What allowed this energy to enter my system?
- Tell me more.

The last "question" ("Tell me more") is for you to simply sit with the energy and ask it to reveal any messages, understandings, or anything else it may want to. This will allow you to receive intuitive information through an open-ended question that you might not otherwise gather. If you are having difficulty trusting your intuition, I suggest moving forward to the *Listening to Intuition* exercise a bit farther in this book. It will allow you to eventually trust the intuitive messages that are arising through questions like these.

When you discern information from these questions, it is always a question if the answers are correct or if you are just "making them up." While some answers you may receive intuitively may not always be 100 percent correct, in asking questions like this you are not typically looking for specific guidance; you are looking for general themes over time. This means that if you are always hearing that you are picking up anger from your office building, that is something to consider, and you may wish to use some cleansing methods on your office, or work with some of the protection methods later described in the book while you are there.

It is also important not to blame sources of "negative" energy. It is likely that even if we are picking up destructive thoughts from a friend that they are not aware that we are absorbing their thoughts or emotions. We can come from a place of compassion for people who might be heavy or destructive in their energy but also have boundaries, and learn to not take that energy on.

The last few questions are not to blame you for taking on any energy. We tend to resonate with specific emotions, thoughts, and experiences in this world. If we personally are in a state of grief, we may find that we tend to pull in the grief of others. If we are a caregiver and nurturer, we may find that we attract "energy vampires," or people who want to take our energy because they can. By discovering these things about ourselves, as well as where we tend to keep them or take them on in our bodies, we can heal, change, and learn how to take care of ourselves energetically so that we can have proper boundaries with others.

Discernment – Part Three

Ideally we will get to a point in our awareness and skill level that we are able to notice energies in our environment before we take them in. Most psychics are "scanners," meaning that they are constantly on guard, looking at all of the people, items, and circumstances in their environment. This leads to a destructive pattern of being consistently on guard as well as not interacting with the environment appropriately. Unskilled psychics tend to shield to protect themselves from the onslaught of stimuli they sense, cutting themselves off from not only "negative" energy but all energy, including beneficial energies. This means that social interaction, healthy nurturing from the environment, and emotional release tend to not flow in and out of our system like they should as long as we remain in this state.

Instead of scanning and shielding we can practice discernment of our environment. Further practice on how to do this for individual people is an intermediate skill that will be developed later in the book. When we enter a room, we can get a sense overall of what is happening in that room. Does it seem chaotic? Peaceful? Does the room seem heavy? Or does it seem light? How do we feel in this room? Sit with this question for a moment and sense if you feel anxiety, a sensation of being closed in on, or if you feel expansive.

Once you have considered the room as a whole, you will consider elements of that room. You do not have to physically scan, but can again ask yourself these questions internally:

- Where in the room is heaviest or has the densest energy?
- Where in the room has the lightest energy?
- Where are there positive or happy emotions in the room?
- Where are there destructive or darker energies in the room?
- Where would be the right place for you to sit, stand, or interact with others?
- Where would be a difficult or negative place for you to sit, stand, or interact with others?
- Is there anyone in the room you should be cautious of?
- Is there anyone in the room you should interact with or feel drawn to?

Although these are simple questions, they can allow us to choose a good seat on the train, to find like-minded people to talk to, and to feel safe in our environment. By properly assessing where we are and the energies of the room consciously, we can allow ourselves to let go a bit. We can lower our defenses and energetically will feel more confident in interacting with others. We can also realize that there may be some people, or some areas of a room or location that we wish to avoid. By allowing ourselves to consciously recognize those energies we can simply avoid them, or realize going in that a situation or person might have more difficult energy, which will prepare us mentally and energetically to interact with them.

Tree Meditation

Many sensitives and psychics have a tendency to disassociate, or stay slightly outside their bodies. This is also true of the general population (we, in general, are not an embodied culture), but as psychics, being out of the body or ungrounded can be enormously detrimental. It is an additional emotional and spiritual issue for many psychics, because they are able to sense the difficult emotions and energies of not only themselves but the world at large, and may not want to be part of the earth. There are whole spiritual communities focused on these types, who would rather be anywhere else than Earth, or in their physical bodies.

No matter what our beliefs are regarding our spiritual origins, we have human bodies for a reason. The world can be a difficult place to live in as a sensitive, but it is even more difficult if we are constantly living in a state of reaction to the people around us, to the spiritual realms, or to the world at large. We must make a conscious choice to be embodied and accept that we are here on Earth, in a human body, and in our current place and time. In making this conscious decision, we can deeply ground ourselves and live a more fulfilling life in our human bodies on Earth.

When most of us take in stimuli, it is through our digestive tract and the energetic channels associated with it. Most of our psychic senses process from top to the bottom, meaning that we receive stimuli from the top half of our body and then try to process it by channeling it through the bottom half of our body. The difficulty with this is that not only do we have weak digestive capabilities but also that we rarely have the channels or energies in our legs open.

In simple terms, we are not grounded or embodied in our lower bodies. In more complex terms, we are intended to process energy both from the top down (Heavens to Earth) energetically but also from the bottom up (Earth to Heavens). When we lack these energetic pathways we feel disjointed, out of balance, and out of place in the world. When psychics lack these pathways, they are unable to process the huge amount of stimuli coming in properly and can get quite physically and emotionally out of balance.

We have a full circuit of energy when we are able to feel a clear pathway of energy flowing down through our bodies, from above our heads and down through our feet into the earth, then energy coming up through the earth into our bodies and into our heads and beyond. At first this feels like two separate streams (above the head moving down and from the earth moving up), but in time, it forms a circuit of continual energy that gives us vitality. This energy is able to properly process and take care of any stimuli coming in, no matter how large. If we are able to get this proper energetic exchange occurring, our health, vibrancy, and emotional stability will dramatically improve.

We often get stimuli stuck in our digestive tract because, as psychics, we simply are not able to digest the sheer volume of material that enters our bodies. Much of this is because we lack the appropriate channels, or pathways, to dispose of energy coming in.

When we begin to ask "Is this mine?" we can start to let go of that which is not ours, as if through the roots of a tree, as in the following exercise.

MEDITATION: Tree Meditation – Part One

Begin with this *Tree* meditation until it feels comfortable:

- Sit or stand in a comfortable position.
- Allow yourself to feel your feet on the floor.
  - If this is all you can do for now, this is wonderful. If you can feel your feet make grounded contact with the floor/earth, continue.
- As you bring gentle focus to your feet, imagine roots coming out of the bottoms of your feet into the earth.
- Grow the roots down as far as you can into the earth.
  - Gradually you should be able to not only imagine the roots going into the earth but have the felt sense of them doing so as well.

MEDITATION: Tree Meditation – Part Two

After you are able to feel your roots growing into the earth, continue:

- With your root system, begin to bring in energy from the earth.
  - This can be any color or texture, although many people choose blue or water, dirt colors, or other earth tones.
  - You are welcome to choose whatever resonates with you and whatever feels right in the moment or on the day you are do-ing this. Choose what your body really feels like it needs. Does it need dirt? Does it need water? Does it need fire from the core of the earth?
- Allow this energy to move up your body as far as it is able.
  - Do not force anything. Simply allow it to flow up as much as it wants.
  - Gradually, it will flow up and through your whole body until it flows out of the top of your head. Do not force this. Let it do this in its own time.
- Now, allow whichever energy is ready to flow down through your body and into the earth through your root system.
  - Do not force anything. Simply direct your body to allow whichever energy is ready to flow from your own body into the earth.

- You can picture the energy leaving your body as a color, or a texture.

Over time your body will recognize these pathways and the flow through them will become permanent. Starting out, this may be quite difficult, as many psychics are really ungrounded and quite "top-heavy" in their energy. This meditation can be done once or twice a day. In the beginning, doing it outside in nature, such as next to a physical tree, can be helpful.

Authentic Self

We all have access to our authentic self, who we vitally are as people and as spiritual beings. When we are overwhelmed by psychic stimuli, or have lost our sense of who we are due to our psychic abilities, it is essential to remember who we are at our core. When we know who we authentically are we are better able to discern what is not "us" and what is not ours. Many psychics are so sensitive they do not have any sort of baseline for who they truly are. Without this understanding though, it is harder to define what is not "us," and to protect ourselves from the impacts of outside stimuli. It is also harder to maintain boundaries, self-esteem, and self-worth, and to develop the type of power and capabilities that will allow us to have an impact in this world.

Connecting with our authentic selves means that we have a safe place within that is healed, vibrant, and healthy. When we are in a situation that is highly emotionally charged or traumatizing, for example, we can return to ourselves and who we know ourselves to be at our core to stop being overwhelmed, stop energy from being drained from us, and maintain boundaries. Over time, this understanding of our authentic selves can allow us to naturally emanate who we are in the world, and we will be naturally protected with appropriate boundaries in all of our interactions.

Our Authentic Self is called different things in different traditions. It can be called the Divine Self, the Inner Physician, the True Self, the Inner God. However we define it, it is us at our best. It is the healed, powerful, and divine aspect of ourselves that is unique, beautiful, and stands in its own power. No matter how lost we may feel, no matter what traumas we have endured, we are spiritually whole, and all of us have this Authentic Self that can be cultivated to effect tremendous healing in our lives.

MEDITATION: Authentic Self

> First, imagine a place that you consider special, where you really felt alive. Typically, this will be a place out in nature, but it can be anywhere. Imagine everything about this place with all of your senses. Make it as vivid as you can.
>
> Next, you are going to imagine your Authentic Self there. Don't overthink this. Simply ask for who you truly are to be there. Notice everything about yourself in this situation. What qualities do you have? Peaceful, happy, powerful, strong?
>
> Say an internal "hello" to your Authentic Self. Introduce yourself. Although this may feel strange the first time you do it, ask her (or him) directly if there is anything that you should know. If you hear something, that is wonderful. If you do not, you can always come back and ask again another time.
>
> Ask your Authentic Self what they would need to come into being into the world. Again, listen for the answer. Say "thank you" to your Authentic Self.
>
> When you are ready, you are going to come back to your current self. When it feels like the right time to do, slowly imagine the Authentic Self merging with you. Basically, you are going to bring the energy and image of the place and the true self into your physical body. Let it fill up your physical body. Sit with it for a while.

You may notice that this may take some work, or it may happen right away. Over time, the Authentic Self may unfold from inside you instead of being external and merging. The Authentic Self, or where you see it, may change, but in time, it will become a permanent fixture inside you. You will be able to act powerfully and authentically, from a place of realizing wholeness and your own power and capabilities in this world.

When we know who we are, we can more easily know what is affecting us that is not inherently "us." The more easily we identity our Authentic Self, the easier it becomes to do the *Is This Mine?* meditation. The more we become who we are truly meant to be in this world, the more we can view our sensitivities as a source of strength and beauty instead of a detriment. Energetically, the more we fully become ourselves, the less space there is for anything that is not "us" to enter our physical bodies or energetic space.

This *Authentic Self* meditation can be done at any time. It is perfect for when you are feeling weak, sick, out of sorts, overwhelmed, or simply would like to feel stronger. The more you do the *Authentic Self* meditation, the more you will be able to stay in your power. Being "in your power" means that you understand who you are and what you are doing in this world. When you know who you are, anything that is not you will automatically be separated out. When you gain access to your Authentic Self and your power, you begin to go from a state of constant overstimulation and reaction to a state of noticing. Things do not affect you as deeply and severely as they once did. There is no space for anything that is not you, and anything that does manage to come in can be separated out by asking, "Is this mine?" and using the *Tree* meditation above to let go of it.

Listening to Intuition

We all have an inner voice and a sense of knowing within ourselves. Our outer culture has allowed us to believe that our feelings, our sense of knowing, and our gut instincts are not as important as a sense of logic or understandings built upon what we were taught by others. As a result, psychic or not, most of us have lost confidence in our inner natures and what our intuition is telling us.

But we can re-establish our connection to our intuition, learn how to work with it, and more importantly, begin to have confidence in ourselves and what we know to be true in this world on a deep level.

Our sense of knowing, or claircognition, is the most common psychic sensitivity. By learning to work with this sense of knowing we can "check in" with facets of our lives and learn what our intuition has to say about them. By learning to establish a relationship with your inner self, or intuition, you will learn how to better manage and appreciate your psychic abilities and what information they have to offer.

This exercise, as is true of many of the meditations and exercises in this book, may need to be repeated a few times before you feel comfortable with it. You are exploring your relationship with yourself, and as with any relationship, spiritual or not, you cannot expect to have a deep relationship right away. You would not expect to have trust, confidence, and rapport with someone you have just said "hello" to once in yoga class or in the grocery store; the same is true of developing spiritual relationships, even if it is a relationship to ourselves. I suggest you do this exercise once a day at first. As you deepen your relationship with yourself, you will soon find that you can quickly check in with your intuition throughout the day. On some days our intuition may be chatty and clear, while on others, we may not be able to sense our intuition, no matter how hard we look for it or want to connect. This is normal. If you are having difficulty, simply try again later that day or on another day. It is also normal for our intuition to block certain information from us. This is because we may not be ready to hear something consciously. For example, I have worked with plenty of women and men whose intuition was screaming at them to get out of their relationship or marriage, and they were not ready to consciously hear that. It simply may not be the right time for us to know something.

So have a bit of patience with yourself, and know that the more you are able to connect with this aspect of yourself, the stronger it becomes.

MEDITATION: Connecting to Your Intuition – Part One

- There is a place in your body where your intuition lives. As you do a gentle body scan, starting at your feet and going up to your head, and down your arms, ask for your body to highlight or show you where your intuition is located in your physical body.
- When you find this place, just bring a bit of focus to this area.
- If your intuition were a color, what would it be?
- Allow yourself to see a light with this color in the area of your body where your intuition lives.
- Simply sit with this colored light, and ask for it to gently expand and heighten so you can really see it. For some of you, it may expand past the boundary of your physical body, or shine more brilliantly, or change color. For others, it may allow for some emotions to arise. If it remains the same, know that even accessing your intuition is a wonderful life-changing step to take.
- Acknowledge that this light is here, and that it is your intuition.

You may choose to stay with simply getting to know your intuition, feeling and sensing it within your body and allowing for it to gently expand. When it feels right to you to continue, you can begin to develop a relationship with it.

MEDITATION: Connecting to Your Intuition – Part Two

- Connect to the light of your intuition.
- Say an internal "hello" to your intuition.
- Ask your intuition directly (like you are speaking to another person, but you can do this internally) if there is anything you should know. Keep things general at first.

- If there is a specific area of your life you are questioning, ask about that situation, such as, "Intuition, can you tell me what I should do about my career?"
- Listen for the answers.
- Say "thank you" when you are done.

Although this is specifically set up to be simple, complications can arise, especially at first. Your intuition may say something to you that doesn't make any sense, such as a single-word answer, or express an image as a response. For example, you might ask what you need to do to feel better about yourself and to develop better self-esteem and hear the answer "Love." In this case, you would then ask how you should go about this, or who might need love, or to be loved? You would continue to ask for clarity until you understand what is being said to you.

You also may reach an impasse, where an answer is not arising for you, or your intuition seems stuck in some way. By asking the question, "If you did have an answer, what would that be?," the intuition can frequently come up with something, even if it did not have an answer before. You may also receive an image with no words; in which case, you can simply note the image and ask for further information about it from your intuition.

Your intuition can be cultivated to the point where you can ask questions about anything, from deep spiritual insights to what top looks better on you in the store. Although it seems silly to ask questions about your day, it is in fact by doing so that you can strengthen your intuition and begin to trust it more. Our intuition is like a muscle—the more we use it and develop it the stronger it becomes, and the more confidence we have in it. So starting by asking questions about which movie you should watch, what you should have for dinner, or what you should do about the difficult person at work. This is the perfect way to start listening to your intuition.

NOTE: Just because we hear something from our intuition, this does not mean that we need to act on it. But by simply acknowledging what we hear, we can develop a good relationship with our intuition. If our intuition is telling us to leave our family and move to Hawaii, we do not need to do so. If our intuition suggests something to us, it becomes conscious for us, and we can then rely on our other senses in order to decide how to proceed in our daily lives.

To clarify this point still further, here is another example.

We might ask our intuition, "What should I do about my health?" and hear the answer, "Exercise." We might then ask, "Can you give me more information about that?" and hear the answer that we should be exercising thirty minutes every day. In reality, we may not be able to do that, either because of our schedules or because we are so out of shape that thirty minutes of exercise every day would cause us real, physical harm. However, we can acknowledge that we need exercise in our lives and convey that back to our intuition by saying, "I hear that I need to exercise, and I acknowledge that." We might then offer what seems like an appropriate compromise solution for us, such as, "I will go for a walk three times a week."

It is normal to distrust the information you are receiving from your intuition, especially at first. We live in a culture where our health, our mental, physical, emotional, and spiritual wellness, and even our spiritual understandings and explorations are divorced from our self-knowledge, intuitive senses, and direct experiences of the world. Sources outside ourselves teach us what to eat, who to be, and about our spiritual nature. While some guidance is necessary, of course, this reliance on external sources of knowledge has caused many of us to distrust any inner guidance or sense of knowing we receive via our intuition.

Know that the answers you receive from your intuition are not set in stone and you do not need to act on them. It is simply information for you to think about. If you get the "wrong" answer, you will eventually get the "right" one—as long as you develop your intuition.

Eventually, your intuition will become a permanent aspect of you, a guiding light in your body and in your life. By trusting and working with your intuition, even if it is a simple daily visualization of this light and a direct "Hello. Is there anything I should know?," you will be well on your way to establishing an important connection. This also means that when we walk into a room that seems "off" to us, we can ask our intuition for reasons why. Or if we get a sense that we should take another route to work we now have an inner resource with answers, connecting our natural, gut instincts with conscious knowledge.

This connection is important, because many of the psychic stimuli we receive are subconscious and our intuition often throws up red flags to get us to notice something about our lives. By developing and working with our intuition, we will be more firmly embodied and connected with our spiritual nature, so that when we have times of overwhelm, or just something strange happening spiritually, we can simply ask about it.

Our intuition is our strongest spiritual ally. Through it, we can learn everything we could want to know about our lives, who we are, and how to work with sensitivities and psychic abilities.

Coming to an Agreement

Once we have begun to develop a relationship with our intuition, we may wish to begin asking it for things that we need. Our intuition is largely in the realm of our subconscious, meaning that it is processing information that is far beyond our capacity to consciously recall. If we were aware of everything that we subconsciously were processing, it would be overwhelming to the point of us being nonfunctional in our daily lives.

In many cases I compare the experience of a sensitive person to watching too many televisions at once. A sensitive may feel sometimes as if they are watching two or five televisions at once, while a highly sensitive person may feel as if they are watching fifty or two hundred televisions at once.

This is a lot of input, and there are times, as discussed in the previous chapters, where the influx of sensory input is so much that it becomes difficult for someone who is psychic to function. Although it sounds exceedingly simple, intuition is a tool that really does work. In cases of overwhelm, or just in general, we can tap into our intuition and simply ask for our subconscious to give us the night off.

We can also ask to not receive so many stimuli consciously. We can do this by "coming to an agreement," meaning that we can access our intuition through the previous work and directly ask the light or our intuition to cut down our conscious awareness of and participation in so many stimuli.

If we feel as if we are watching twelve televisions at once, we can ask for it to cut down to six. If we feel resistance to cutting down to six televisions (either from ourselves or other sources), we can ask for it to cut down to eight, and see how that feels. Similar to other calibrating methods in this book, we can choose a number that feels right to us and continue to ask for the amount of material coming at us that we are consciously aware of to cut down or to come at us in a gentler way that we can process more appropriately.

One of the biggest difficulties for most psychics is sleep—either somnolence (sleeping too much), insomnia, or strange dreams that make us feel wiped out instead of refreshed. By asking for a night off from our intuition before bed we can significantly, if not completely, cut down on the amount of issues that we have during the sleep cycle.

There is often some resistance to this exercise due to its simplicity as well as the fact that being so sensitive is often a part of the psychic's identity. By realizing that we do not have to constantly be "on" and that we will always receive the information that is necessary, even if we negotiate our conscious awareness down a level, we can come into an agreement with our body, with our subconscious, and with our intuition that allows for us to have times of diminished conscious awareness.

We all live in a sea of information, and even the most sensitive of us only have an awareness of some of it. When we are exhausted, ill, or struggling, there is no reason for us to not come to this agreement. It will allow us to come more into our physical bodies, get the rest we need, and take care of our physical health instead of constantly being vigilant or fighting against stimuli coming our way from the outside.

Most psychics benefit from focusing more on their physical health, embodiment, and individual emotional, energetic, and spiritual needs. By asking our intuition and subconscious to reduce the conscious stimuli we receive, we can change the focus in our lives and make sense of what we have already experienced, as well as our own physical, mental, energetic, and spiritual health.

EXERCISE: Focusing the Televisions – Part One

In some cases, asking for the night off or using the simplified version of "Coming to an Agreement" may not be quite the right tool for us. This is most often because we are in such a state of overwhelm that we cannot imagine ourselves being in a state of rest or calm. This may also be because of our level of sensitivity. While it is popularly thought that psychics can simply ask for their abilities to "go away," this is often not the case for moderately or highly psychic individuals.

In cases like this we often need to focus, rather than asking for psychic stimuli to simply cease or cut down. To do this we will first take a few simple breaths in and out. This will help to calm the nervous system. You will then visualize or sense the psychic information coming your way as if there were television screens in front of you. Note how many televisions there may be. One? Five? Twenty? Five hundred? How many different types of stimuli or disparate pieces of information are coming your way to be processed? Keep in mind that this number may change each time you do this exercise.

Now you will ask your intuition to allow you to focus on the one or two television screens that you should be focused on. The other televisions that are "on" should reduce to static or turn off. If your focus turns to a few television screens, allow it to gradually focus on just one.

Now, note the information coming through. What is the scene in this television? What is this specific piece of stimuli that is coming through trying to tell you? Allow yourself to fully sense whatever is coming through that television screen.

If you are not a visual person, you can still create a felt sense of this. This means that you can feel or otherwise sense the amount of static—such as from a television that is on an "off" channel—reduce, and then use your other senses (such as a sense of knowing or your intuition) to focus and find out which television you should "focus" on.

By focusing, you will find that the end result is that you feel more relaxed, less overwhelmed, and can begin to sort out the information coming through to you in a way that is helpful to you. This is one of the key steps in learning how to process the stimuli coming toward you and will eventually allow you to discern what sort of psychic information you pick up with clarity.

EXERCISE: Focusing the Televisions — Part Two

No matter how sensitive or psychic we are, we are only consciously aware of a portion of the vast sea of stimuli that surrounds us. It is typical for sensitives to react to not only conscious material but also subconscious material. Part One of this exercise was focused primarily on conscious material—material that we sense is coming our way. In this instance, the televisions would be "on," such as a television that is actively broadcasting a show.

In the first example, we may have twenty televisions that are playing twenty different programs at once. But we will also have many televisions that are playing static, or are no longer playing shows, similar to how some televisions do late at night or very early in the morning. It is likely that for a psychic person with a high sensitivity level that they may have many televisions playing shows, as well as many more televisions showing static, or giving us psychic stimuli that we are either not fully aware of or are not focused on.

Instead of focusing on the televisions that are simply "on," you will instead ask to see or sense televisions that are both giving you conscious as well as subconscious material (or both "on" and static, respectively). This may be a huge row of televisions, or many rows of televisions.

Note how many televisions approximately are there. Now, note how many are "on" versus on a channel with static. You do not need to be exact with this; a rough estimate works fine.

You will now focus only on the televisions that are showing static. Intend that these televisions, or a majority of them, go to the "off" position. These screens should go blank, and some of the televisions should disappear altogether.

You will now go back and work with the "on" televisions, focusing on one or two screens as we did in the first part of this exercise. If you are having difficulty, you may now find that an intermediary step of having the television that was "on" turn to static is helpful. You may also find after working with this exercise for a while that focusing on an individual television and asking for it to turn "on" from the "off" or static position will allow you to fine-tune your psychic sensibilities and receive information in a much more focused way. It is also true that when we allow ourselves to focus on a television that is already on, we will allow ourselves to more readily understand the input that is coming our way, which increases our chances of processing it through other methods, such as the *Tree* meditation.

Developing a Psychic Library

We all filter things differently. Let's say that two people who are exactly the same in terms of psychic abilities (for example, moderately sensitive, both at 97 percent, meaning only 3 percent of the population is more sensitive than they are) step into a room. They are going to receive information differently, not only because they may have different psychic sensitivities (one may be more open in terms of hearing (clairaudience); the other dominantly takes in information like a sponge as an empath) but also because of their life experiences and personal history.

We all have different experiences of this world, different joys and traumas that have been a part of our path. One person may love ice cream cake because their parents got them one for every birthday when they were growing up. The person next to them may hate ice cream cake for the same reason. Different parents, different birthdays, different associations from their individual histories.

All of our experiences in this world make a framework for how we process energy. Put simply, one person may look at a house and think it is pretty, and the other person who has studied architecture may look at the same house and notice that it is a gothic house from the 1850s and comment on the use of a steeply pitched roof to accent the turrets and bays.

This can be extended to everything that we process psychically. We have been taught standardized reasoning and procedures by people who are not psychic (or perhaps only mildly psychic); therefore, such people would focus on facts, such as specific colors are associated with individual chakras; if you see the color blue, spiritually it means this; if you see this particular animal, it has this particular spiritual significance; if you have an issue with your thyroid, it is due to a specific spiritual or emotional dysfunction. We love one-to-one ratios in our culture. This way, it is easy to look up a dream, an animal, or a spiritual experience and pretend that it is standardized.

But this is not how psychic abilities or sensitivities actually work. While specific symbols, archetypes, images, colors do have spiritual connotations, and generalities can be made about specific spiritual experiences or psychic stimuli, we are each different in terms of how these stimuli filter through our senses.

This means that although 51 percent of people (a majority) may look up what that spider means in their spiritual animal directory, and have it speak to them based on common symbols and experiences in this world, the other 49 percent looking up that same material would not find any personal meaning in that experience.

So to work with your psychic abilities, one of the most important things you can do is to build a sort of "psychic library." To do this, all you need to do is buy a notebook (unless you have a really good memory) and work with your intuition, as discussed in the previous exercise, and start to write out what your personal psychic library is.

EXERCISE: Creating a Psychic Library

When you are ready, you will simply begin to note how you receive psychic input. At first, keep this simple:

- *Do you tend to see things?* Do you see things through internal vision, or externally? (Basically, do you see them as you would your coffee table? Or do you just sense that it is there?)

- *Do you hear things?* When you hear things, do you have acute hearing, such as being able to hear things from far away? Or do you hear things that other people do not? Do you hear other people's thoughts?
- *Do you smell things?* For example, from farther away, such as the steakhouse down the road? Are you able to pick up nuances that others do not, such as which ingredients are in a dish? Are you smelling things that are not physically there?
- *Do you tend to feel things?* What do you tend to feel? Emotions? How a place feels? How people are feeling? How is your sense of feeling focused?
- *Do you sense things?* Health information? How a person is doing, or what masks they wear? Do you sense when people are lying? Can you sense things from people, animals, the environment? Which part of the environment? Trees, rocks, sky?
- *Do you know things?* What do you get a sense of knowing about? World events, events in your life before they happen, spiritual information without knowing how?

There are other senses, and we can certainly go into more depth with these, but it is extremely beneficial to take some time and write down some general thoughts about the nature of your psychic abilities. Knowing how you take in information—beyond, for example, just simply calling yourself an empath—will allow you to understand your individual abilities and how they present.

As has been mentioned, even under the heading of empathic abilities, the individual abilities are likely to vary wildly from person to person. One may pick up more information from people while another from world or local events, and still another will be highly reactive to the weather. By understanding how you are individually calibrated, and sitting with your own abilities for a bit and taking notice of what exactly you notice around you and how you notice it, you can begin to build your own "psychic library."

The second part of this exercise involves paying attention to what specifically you notice through your own unique sensitivities. Do you tend to hear bells? Do you tend to see the color blue? Focus on what shows up for you a lot, not as a one-off. For example, as psychics, we may have a one-time experience of hearing the thoughts of a person across from us. Something experienced once, or a few times, is interesting, but it should not be the focus of our psychic library. If we constantly are seeing blue flashing lights around us, however, we should take note. If we see spirits, what do they look like to us? What are the different ways in which we see them?

Write down what you tend to see, sense, hear, taste, and so forth on a regular basis. Once you have noted not only how you tend to process things but also your most common experiences, you are on your way to developing your own unique psychic library.

After having done this, the next time you have a psychic experience that is typical for you, make a general note of how it makes you feel. Good? Bad? Neither? What is your sense of whatever you are seeing or sensing? Good? Bad? Neither?

This is, of course, an oversimplification of things. People tend to bring a lot of fear into their spiritual encounters, and to their abilities in general. It is entirely typical for someone in a state of overwhelm, for example, to react to any sort of spiritual stimuli as if it were evil incarnate. It is also typical for someone to be taught that their psychic abilities are wrong, or just simply not want to deal with them, to react to the entire spirit world as if it is something to be afraid of.

The more knowledge we have, the more we realize that we are only aware of a fraction of stimuli that surrounds us, no matter how sensitive we are. By educating ourselves we can understand that spiritual stimuli is always around us, but only a certain percentage of the population can notice anything that is not crassly physical.

For the purposes of building your library, try to look past your own fears and purely into what you sense within yourself, as well as to whatever the stimuli are on a basic level, noting what emotions and feelings arise.

If you feel really uncomfortable, that is something to note. If you feel more peaceful, that is something also to note. If you are still in a stage of reacting to anything not physical as if it were out to get you, I would suggest returning to some of the exercises we have already covered, such as the *Authentic Self* meditation, as well as going forward to the Spiritual Hygiene section of this book. Do that work until you feel more prepared to move into understanding what you are sensing.

Once you get a basic sense of the spiritual stimuli you are receiving, connect to your intuition and ask what it is. Pick one stimulus (for example, you are seeing a blue light), and every time you notice it, see how it makes you feel and ask your intuition what it means. Now begin to sense variations in this stimulus. For example, sometimes you may notice a large blue light, or a flashing blue light, or occasionally a blue-and-yellow light. Again, go through the process of seeing how it makes you feel, your basic reaction to it, and asking your intuition what it means.

This is how you build a "psychic library" and begin to understand how you filter information individually. A large blue light may be a very different spiritual presence than a blinking small blue-and-yellow light. Over time, what will happen is that you will understand that, for example, the large blue light is an angelic protector, and that every time you see the blinking light it means that one of your children is upset. By going through each of your common experiences, and how they differ, you will build your "psychic library" and understand what you are actually seeing or sensing. In turn, this will drastically change how you react to spiritual stimuli.

It is normal to experience variations in what we sense. For example, on the face of it, seeing a blue light seems simple. However, if we notice something more complex, such as seeing spirits, things might require us to do a bit more work to build our psychic library appropriately. What does it mean that we are seeing a spirit that is just shadow with no features? Or someone who has features but is all gray? Or a ball of energy with no form? Sensing a spirit but are not able to see it?

By breaking things down and approaching each stimulus as a separate phenomenon, we can feel more in control of our experiences and understand what is going on. We make a note of each occurrence, what it is, when it tends to occur (for example, noting what time of day, what we are doing, what may be going on in our lives when it appears), then we ask our intuition about its meaning. Not only does this approach drastically reduce any associated fear—a natural reaction in unskilled psychics to approaching the unknown—but it also shows us how we react emotionally, physically, and spiritually to such stimuli.

In this manner, we can understand when we need to react out of fear (and perhaps do spiritual bathing or cleansing from the energetic hygiene chapter) and when a comforting presence or a simple sign is coming through to us.

CHAPTER FOUR

Working with Psychic Abilities – Intermediate Skills

Before starting to work with intermediate skills, I suggest that you gain a basic sense of who you are through the *Authentic Self* meditation, as well as a solid understanding and fluency in the *Is This Mine?* meditation. Although you certainly can proceed before that time, you will more easily develop the skills in this chapter if you have a certain level of competency with the more basic skills.

The Basic Skills chapter was focused on understanding who you are, differentiating what is not yours, and beginning to develop trust and understanding of how you individually process or filter things as a psychic; the Intermediate Skills chapter is focused on more directly working with spiritual stimuli and how we receive it in our physical bodies. By learning how to work with our nervous system (how our spiritual systems take energy into our physical bodies) and properly interface with spiritual energies, we become more skilled in managing our abilities.

Every step we take to regulate how we interface with spiritual energies allows our skills to develop. The more skill we develop, the less overwhelmed and more empowered we feel about our psychic abilities, rather than believing them to be a detriment to our lives. For this reason, I suggest that the work in this chapter should be done gradually, allowing your skill level to grow in your own time.

Scattered Energy

It is typical for psychics to have a wide field of perception. Many psychics are out of their bodies, or simply have large energetic fields, meaning that they take in a lot of information and do not have distinct boundaries. This creates a situation where our energy is scattered and we are not centered in our physical bodies.

When our energy is scattered, we feel ungrounded, not ourselves, or unable to think or process energy appropriately. We may feel foggy, cloudy, or dizzy, or like our nervous systems are constantly in a state of alarm, or "fight or flight," because we are reaching out our feelers and energetically going outside our bodies to assess, scan, and react to energy coming at us.

This meditation allows us to gather that scattered energy and return to our bodies, where we feel more solid and grounded in our physical natures. Over time, we also may find that our thoughts, anxieties, and signs of overwhelm and overstimulation calm down. The result is good sleep, a peaceful nature, and an ability to function better in our daily lives.

MEDITATION: Scattered Energy

I would like you to sit in a quiet place and imagine an egg shape surrounding you. Imagine the boundaries of this egg—depending on your perception, and how wide your energy field is, it will be 3-12 inches away from your physical body and wider at the top, by the crown of your head, and narrower under your feet. If you are not able to sense this egg, it is likely that you are too open, so for now, simply imagine this egg surrounding you.

Now ask to see or sense the scattered energy that is around you— it will look or feel like electricity. Based on your perceptions, you may sense, feel, smell, or notice it in other ways; it may, for example, present itself as shapes, a color, or a scent. However you perceive your scattered energy in the egg surrounding you is fine.

Ask to be further shown which energy in your egg is actually yours. Imagine it as a different kind of light, or sense it in a different manner than energy that simply just surrounds you that might not be yours.

Now collect this energy—you can imagine it just coming into you, or you can physically scoop it up. Trust your intuition on this. Some people breathe it in. When it comes in, allow it to gather in your center, at your midline (basically the whole spine from your sacrum/ tailbone all the way up to your head both front and back).

Breathe out through your mouth three times or more to end the meditation. You can then begin the *Authentic Self* meditation, or go about your day.

In time, you may realize that your energy has scattered farther than 3-12 inches around you. You can gently ask that any of this scattered energy be willing to return to your egg, so that you can more easily sense it. You will want this energy to return to your egg first, rather than directly into your physical body, so that you can carry out the step of determining which part of this energy is in fact yours.

I suggest always asking for energy to return willingly, because there may be very good reasons that our energy has scattered. We tend to scatter energetically in response to overwhelm or trauma, and there may be parts of us that need the support of an experienced spiritual worker (who can do something like Soul Retrieval) in order for our energy to return.

The more that we work with the energy that has scattered that is willing to return, the less scattered and the more whole we become. Over time, this exercise will allow you to return a great deal of energy that is likely outside your body, and will also allow you to sense when you are scattered so that you can take steps to work with it. By this, I simply mean that if we spend our whole lives being scattered, dispersed, and out of body, it is hard to realize or acknowledge when we are slightly more scattered than usual. When we are more in our bodies, with more of our energy in and around us, we gain a baseline understanding of what it feels like to be "home," and we can more easily tell when we are scattered, or not "home."

This exercise is a simple, gradual way to alleviate fatigue, feel more embodied, and begin to understand our own unique energy dynamics. In time, this tool becomes fairly simple. You see, feel, or sense energy that has scattered around you. You question what is yours (always do this, as there is a lot of stuff around you that is likely not yours). You imagine it as a color or a unique type of electric current, then you bring it back in, feel it in your midline, and take a few breaths.

Whenever you are feeling scattered, as if you are overthinking or are feeling overwhelmed, reclaiming the energy that has scattered into your midline will really help. You can do it with or without the *Authentic Self* meditation. You can do it in public, during confrontations with family members, or when you are feeling overwhelmed by the amount of stimuli around you. Having a solid understanding of this exercise will help to develop further tools, such as Opening.

Opening

Depending on the day or our sensitivity level, we may have a huge number of stimuli coming our way that is not ours. In the beginning this can be overwhelming, and we are likely uncertain of where things are coming from, doubt ourselves with what information is coming across, or are submerged in so many stimuli that it is difficult to discern what is going on around us clearly.

One of the ways we can work with this is through the practice of Opening. Opening means that you are expanding yourself briefly in order to more fully realize the messages, images, scents, sensory information, or whatever else is coming your way. We do this for several reasons: to understand what is around us clearly; to connect with spirits, beings, angels, and other energies that can teach or help us; to connect with ancestors clearly; and for other reasons—for example, people who work as professional psychics may do this to open up even more to their surroundings in order to learn more about them.

When faced with sensitivities we tend to retract energetically from our environments, shielding ourselves, causing blockages, and creating boundaries in order to protect ourselves. Although it sounds natural to want to shut down, or retract our energy in the face of overwhelm or while working with psychic abilities, in general, the most effective solution in most cases (with a few notable exceptions discussed during the Shielding and Sealing sections) is to actually open, or expand.

Retraction and stagnation are painful. They create physical and emotional pain and cause stimuli to not process properly. They cause us to shut down not only to harmful, toxic, or difficult stimuli but also to shut down in general to our lives, and to anything good coming our way. By opening we can have clear energy pathways, clear boundaries, and not suffer the consequences that come from shielding, retracting, or closing down, such as fatigue, pain, and overwhelm.

When we allow ourselves to open, we can clearly find out what is in our environment. We can then close and take the steps necessary to work with it—to protect ourselves, to clear the stimuli, or to learn.

MEDITATION: Structures of Opening

- Picture your midline. Your midline, front and back, goes from the tip of your tailbone all the way up and to the middle of your head. It will basically divide you into two halves (two sides, left and right).

- Sit for a moment with this midline and feel energy start to settle here. We will work with this more in the future, but for now just feel yourself settle into your midline.
- Directly in the center of your head, in your brain, is the area that is associated with your "third eye," as it is known in spiritual literature; in anatomy and physiology, it is known as the pineal gland, but in reality comprises the pineal gland, pons, midbrain, and third and fourth ventricles of the brain. You do not need to know physiology for this. Trust me, you will find it. If you are having difficulty, just find the center of your head.
- At the end of our spinal cord in the back of our neck is the brain stem. This is one of our more sensitive receiving areas in our body, it is known as a "spirit gate" (more on this later).
- Feel the entire "opening" continuum—sacrum/tailbone, spine (both front and back) and midline, going up into the brain stem and into the middle of the head. In the middle of the head, picture a round ball of light illuminated. Feel this entire continuum lit up like a flagpole (from tip of sacrum/tailbone just above the anus all the way to the middle illuminated ball in the head).

How to Open

- Settle in and feel comfortable with wherever you are sitting or lying down.
- Gently focus on this continuum from the tailbone all the way to the center of the head.
- Feel or sense the illuminated ball in the middle of the head.
- Now you are going to picture a gate, a door (I typically suggest a door) or some other structure covering the brain stem (back of the neck) and inside the middle of the head (pineal gland/third eye). These are two separate doors. In time, these will be permanent structures.
- Picture these doors closed. The illumination and feelings of brightness should stop or slow down.
- Now allow these doors to open. Allow light to stream out, and for the entire illumination process to occur, of midline and up, through these doors.
- Now allow this light to expand as far as it can past your physical body into your environment.

- As you are doing this, say internally that you are opening.
- When you are done, picture the light coming back into your mid-line, back past the doors, and you shutting the doors. The light is still there but it is now behind closed doors.

NOTE: If you are hesitant about performing this *Opening* meditation, you can always ask spirit guides, the divine, or other protectors to keep an eye on things and keep you safe. You may also choose to take a salt bath afterward.

Understandably, people are cautious when performing this *Opening* meditation the first few times. Most of us who are psychic likely have spent a great deal of time hiding or stopping stimuli the best we can, and the idea of opening more to it can make us a bit apprehensive. But it is through accessing our light through this continuum above that we can begin to access more of our Authentic Selves. This can allow us to naturally understand who we are, as well as protect ourselves.

In addition, Opening is one of the key things that will allow you to open and close to the stimuli that are around you. In time, you can feel this continuum, open the doors, and have your spiritual senses heighten. You can also close down your senses in dangerous or difficult situations without causing harm to yourself, such as erecting shields tends to do over time. After opening and closing the midline, we can further advance to working with the Spirit Gates themselves.

Spirit Gates

Spirit Gates are structures associated with several chakras, mainly the first (root) and second (sacral), fourth (heart), sixth (third eye), and seventh (crown) chakras. In addition, there are spirit gates in the back of the skull, loosely associated with the sixth (third eye) chakra, and above our heads and below our feet.

Main Spirit Gates

The main spirit gates are the first and second chakras (root and sacral), fourth (heart) chakra, and the back of the head. It's important to work with these spirit gates first before working with the more advanced spirit gates, such as the spirit gates above the crown of the head.

The Sacral Spirit Gate is associated with the first and second chakra and is located between the kidneys. It is also associated with the sacrum, or tailbone itself. It is a large, circular energy that goes all the way from the center of the sacrum to approximately just behind the belly button (where the kidneys typically are). The Heart Spirit Gate is located in the back of the heart, and the Head Spirit Gate is located where the back of the neck meets the base of the head, and is associated with the "back" of the third eye chakra. Each spirit gate can be shut and quite small or can be quite large. These spirit gates are present in everyone, even if they are not psychic or sensitive.

The minor spirit gates are located in the third eye (between the eyebrows), crown (direct center of the head going upward), below the feet, at the crown (apex of the head) and above the head, and in the center of the palmar side of the hands and soles of the feet. The minor spirit gates are present in every one of us but are only activated, or engaged, in certain psychic individuals.

Spirit gates are how information of a spiritual nature comes through to us. Although they somewhat correspond to the chakras and their functions, they are more about our individual sensitivities and how "open" we are to psychic stimuli. While we always want to have a balanced, well-regulated chakra system, we may wish to close or open spirit gates based on how much information is coming at us. Chakras are about how we process stimuli through our physical bodies, through our past experiences and our belief systems. They are storehouses of all of the information from our current lives, past lives, ancestry, society, and even the world that we have not processed or awoken to. Spirit gates are purely about how much information is coming at us from outside sources. They open directly to our greater spiritual nature and any type of spiritual stimulus that surrounds us.

Many psychics do not realize that they have active spirit gates, so they complain about back pain, neck pain, and odd physical sensations as a result of their spirit gates being too open and too much information coming in. If our spirit gates are active, or too open, this means that we are taking in a lot of spiritual information. In the major spirit gates (low back, back of heart, and back of the neck), this can result in feelings of pain, congestion, or of something present in these areas that does not feel like it comes from us. Again, asking the basic question, "Is this mine?" can allow us to discern if there is something present in these areas that is not ours.

Minor psychic gates are only active in psychic individuals. Commonly, the psychic gates in the hands are the most active, as a result of Reiki and other energy healing courses that encourage us to become more receptive through our hands. Although much of the psychic literature focuses on the third eye and crown spirit gates, they are only active in moderately and highly psychic individuals. The spirit gates located above the head and below the feet are rarely activated; they are typically only present in highly psychic people on deep spiritual paths. There are also spirit gates located off the body that allow for other sorts of input to come into our energetic field, but these are only activated in skilled, highly psychic states.

MEDITATION: Main Spirit Gates

Working with the main spirit gates is deceptively simple. During the process of opening, feel for the spirit gates located in the sacrum, back of the heart, and back of the neck. You will work with each spirit gate one by one. I suggest starting out with the low back and moving upward:

- Feel, see, or sense in some manner how these physical areas of your body seem to you. Are they congested? In pain? Or do they feel relaxed or open?

- Ask to sense, see, or feel the amount of energy present in those areas. For beginners, it is typically easier if you imagine energy as a color. Even if you are not a visual person, you can sense a color in this area, or just allow yourself to feel if the area feels hollow or empty, or if it feels stuck, in pain, congested, or anywhere in between. Ask how much of this energy is yours?

- Once you have familiarized yourself with the area, allow yourself to imagine a doorway, gateway, or other opening present in these areas.

- Sense how open it is, how much energy you are allowing through.

- Imagine the doors shutting. Sit with this sensation for a moment. You can do each spirit gate individually, which is often easier at first, or all three of them at once. How do you feel? How does that area feel now?

- Now imagine the doors opening. Sit with this for a moment. If you are not a visual person, you can feel this happening. How does it feel to have one spirit gate open? Or all three spirit gates open?

- Now feel into your midline, as you did during the *Opening* exercise. Feel how the spirit gates interact with your midline.

- Allow the energy of your midline to expel any energy collected that is not yours through the spirit gate, like a whale spout. You can feel this happening or imagine this as a light or color.

- Watch it leave your energy field (the area around you), or get an intuitive sense that it is gone.
- Now return to the doors. Open or close them as much as feels right to you at the moment.

By learning to open and close spirit gates at will you can eventually learn how open or closed feels to you, and what feels right in your daily life. When you feel overwhelmed, check your spirit gates—they may need to close for a while. You may need to put an iron door or shield over them in situations where you feel like you are in danger to protect yourself. You may also want to open them fully to vent anything in them, or to get a better idea of what is going on in your environment or with a person with whom you are interacting.

Any time you place anything over the spirit gates (or anywhere in your body for that matter), such as a shield, please go back and remove it. The spirit gates are intended to allow you to interface with your spiritual self, providing you with information on a spiritual level. Closing them permanently, or shielding them, can lead to pain and other psychological, physical, and spiritual issues.

Minor Spirit Gates

The minor spirit gates in the feet, hands, third eye, and crown can be opened and closed similar to the major spirit gates. The only difference is that they are not active in every individual. Activation means that there is a constant, or fairly constant, sensation of energy in the area. This energy is not only the feeling of your own body energy but of an interface with Spirit, with the divine. Major spirit gates are definitely more active in some of us when we have a higher psychic awareness, but they are present and working in everyone.

Depending on your level of spiritual advancement or skill, you may or may not be able to consciously process the information coming in through the major spirit gates. Minor spirit gates are only activated when it is necessary for them to work, and in most people remain dormant. This means that the crown gets activated when we are open to divine input, or channeling; the third eye, when we are clairvoyant; the hands, for healing or sensory capabilities; and the feet, to interface with Earth energies.

The spirit gates above the head and below the feet are the interface between pure spiritual energy and our energetic field. This energy then goes through the gateway of the crown or the soles of the feet or the perineum and is filtered by our human experiences, belief systems, and so on.

Other minor spirit gates can be activated all around our energy field and number in the dozens. We can work with these minor spirit gates when they are open in order to figure out what they are and where they are leading. Learning to work with closing or opening the main spirit gates listed above can allow us to eventually learn how to control the amount of spiritual stimuli coming our way. If our minor spirit gates awaken, we will begin to understand our relation to divinity on a deeper level, and receive direct spiritual insights from the divine.

When you feel ready to open or work with the minor spirit gates, which is not a necessity or skill that most psychics need to learn to manage their abilities, find an accomplished spiritual teacher who can help you. The closer that we get to advanced material, such as the activation and knowledge of spiritual structures like the minor spirit gates, the easier it is for us to get off balance, or simply require assistance. Working with the major spirit gates is a helpful skill that any sensitive or psychic can and should learn, but learning how to activate and work with the minor spirit gates is not a necessity, unless you are at a point where you are balanced psychologically, have the appropriate teacher, as well as a calling to do so.

Dialing Down the Nervous System

As psychics, we often take in much more stimuli from our environment than we can often handle. This leads to a number of physical symptoms, stemming from an overwhelmed nervous system.

Our nervous system is the first receiver in our physical bodies of spiritual information, and is the interface between our spiritual "bodies" and our physical body. When we are highly sensitive or psychic, we have too much information to process into our physical bodies, and we develop nervous system overload. This leads to a whole host of physical, emotional, and spiritual symptoms, such as inflammation, a feeling of being constantly "on," feelings of being consistently overwhelmed by even the smallest tasks, fatigue, digestive issues, immune system issues, insomnia, hormonal imbalances, heart problems, physical pains in the body, worsening of chronic disease patterns, and an inability to keep proper boundaries.

Our nervous systems need quiet, reflective time, as well as self-nurturing, in order to process the sheer number of stimuli we come across on a daily basis. Self-nurturing may include spending time in a quiet environment with no distractions (including the phone or television); bodywork that is focused on nervous system repair, such as Craniosacral Therapy or Reiki; Acupuncture; an individualized herbal program from an Acupuncturist/Herbalist, an Ayurvedic Practitioner, or a Clinical Herbalist; baths; nature hikes; meditation; and sensory deprivation tanks.

Finding individual ways to destress and prevent your nervous system being so engaged and "on" is crucial to remaining healthy. As we will discuss soon, physical exercise that is appropriate for your nature is also crucial to maintaining a healthy and balanced physical as well as spiritual nature.

Beyond basic self-care mechanisms, learning how to work with your nervous system through imagery or the "felt sense" (what you are feeling in your body) is crucial to your well-being. Although the following exercise is seemingly simple, done correctly and consistently, it can help everything from overall stress levels and emotional stressors to chronic pain to sleep issues.

MEDITATION: Nervous System

> Allow yourself to feel the current stress in your body. The muscle aches, the tightness, pain, stress, discomfort, and other sensations. Within those sensations, there may be a sensation of something that feels "amped up," something that feels overexcited, going too fast, or simply a feeling of anxiety or fear. If you have been in sympathetic overload for a long time, you may instead feel this as a sense of emptiness, overwhelming fatigue, depression, or a molasses-like quality associated with your system being frozen or barely moving.
>
> Sit with this sensation for a moment. If you are able to visualize this background system—the one that is really amped up or is frozen, empty, or too fatigued—do so. Visualize it as a color, a vibration, or a circuit of some sort. Whatever you feel or visualize or get a sense of knowing about while you are carrying out the inquiry portion of this exercise, or any of the others, is wonderful. If you do not feel like the information is right, or you are doubting yourself, know that the more that you work with the skills in the book, the more trust and faith you will have in the answers, and the easier the skills get.
>
> Once you get acquainted with feeling or seeing what your nervous system is like, you can move on. Allow yourself to imagine a dial with numbers going from "1" to "10." A "10" is the most overwhelmed, buzzing, frantic nervous system that you can ever recall in your per-

sonal history. For just a moment, allow yourself to recall this. I realize that this is unpleasant, but recalling a time that you were at a "10" will very clearly show you where you are now and create the "dial" and its parameters in this exercise.

A "1" on the dial is the most empty, frozen, fatigued feeling nervous system you can remember. For just a moment, allow yourself to recall a moment when you experienced this. If you have not experienced this, consider what a "1" would be for you—a time you personally felt lethargic, depressed, or empty. Perhaps right after a severe illness or a bad breakup.

A "5" on the dial is a healthy nervous system. It is not slow, or fast. It is relaxed, you can breathe with ease, there is minimal pain or discomfort, emotions feel smooth, and stress is minimal. Many people experience this on a beach vacation or somewhere similar.

Now that you understand the dial, honestly evaluate where you are on this dial right now. A "6," a "2," an "8," a "3"? As you work with this system, you will get to know what each number means for you, but for now just evaluate to the best of your abilities where you are on this dial.

Once you have picked your number (I will use the number 8) ask yourself what a "7" might look and feel like. Imagine your dial going down to the number 7 as you ask your nervous system if it can move down to that number.

If it moves, that is wonderful. You will feel a change in stress, in your body, in your nervous system. If there is hesitancy on the part of your nervous system in moving down (or up) a whole number, ask for it to move to a "7.5" or a "7.8." Whichever number on the dial your system is ready to move to is perfect. If it does not want to move at all, do not get frustrated, as even realizing where you are on this scale and simply checking in with yourself is enough to effect changes.

Although this is an invaluable exercise, it can take your body a bit to get used to. Once you understand what each of the numbers are, and where you are on the dial through basic inquiry, this exercise will allow you to quickly recalibrate your nervous system to a healthier point on the dial.

It is important to note that if we are at an "8" or a "9," or a "1," "2," or "3," that it is too much to ask for our nervous systems to go straight to a "5," or a healthy, balanced nervous system. By working incrementally over a period of time, even if we go from a "7" on the dial to a "6.75," we can effect the most change.

By honestly asking our nervous system what level it is comfortable stepping down to each time, we can gradually and comfortably come to a new state of calibration. We can also get to know our own symptoms of overload on an individual basis, allowing us to use skills to better navigate our way through, using the "dial" technique and other tools in this book, as well as basic self-care.

Opening the Spiritual Stomach

It is well known to psychics that spiritual overload greatly impacts the digestive system. When we are unskilled or lack knowledge as psychics, this may seem like a strange correlation. We may not understand why our physical bodies are bearing the effects of our sensitivities, or we may not wish to connect the dots about our sensitive nature having an impact on us physically, because we do not know what to do about it. As we become more conscious and questioning (as well as skilled), we begin to understand that the digestive system is unfortunately one of the bigger physical systems in our body to be impacted by psychic abilities.

Our physical bodies not only digest food but all the energy and spiritual stimuli around us. Everything about our day—our thoughts, emotions, and stimuli around us—needs to be processed. Typically, we understand this as a very physical phenomenon. We eat a meal, and it goes into our mouths, down through the esophagus to our stomach, into our large and small intestines, and out of our bodies; our liver, gallbladder, pancreas, and other organs also play a role in this process. The higher sensitivity level that we have, the more information that we have to process through our digestive systems. This eventually leads to overload, and difficulties with not only energy but also the physical digestive process

The abdomen is the center of who we are as people. Our identity and how we feel about ourselves is housed here. In Traditional Chinese Medicine (TCM), careful palpation of the abdomen, or "hara diagnosis," can reveal our patterns of dysfunction or ill health in their entirety. The stomach and digestive tract are referred to as the "second brain"; they reflect our thoughts, contribute to our moods, and reveal how able we are to be in the present moment, as well as how able we are to let things go from our past.

As you may have ascertained, this is a place that is prone to quite a bit of dysfunction, even for non-psychics. It is often essential to go to a holistic health practitioner to figure out physical sources of abdominal discomfort, such as food allergy testing, readjusting of diet, and so forth, as well as meditating to clear our cluttered thoughts so that they do not impact our digestive tract; however, we can also learn how to energetically and spiritually work with our digestive tracts, so that we can properly process the massive amount of energy that comes at us daily. This is called "Opening the Spiritual Stomach."

EXERCISE: Opening the Spiritual Stomach

Many of us who have anatomy training know that the stomach is actually in the upper quadrant of our abdomen, above the belly button and slightly to the left anatomically (if we were looking down at our own abdomen) for most of us. Opening our Spiritual Stomach encompasses the entire abdomen, instead of strictly correlating to anatomical placement.

- Picture a line going down your front midline, from your xiphoid process (the last place you can feel your ribs in the center line) all the way down to your pubic bone.
- Now picture this line floating off your body in exactly the same place, but now 3-6 inches away from your skin.
- Imagine this line is now a zipper, with the slider being at the top.

Now that we have the zipper mechanism, the opening of the Spiritual Stomach, we are going to visualize the rest of it.

The Spiritual Stomach begins approximately 3 inches away from us (this will grow larger and farther away the more we work with it) and looks like a giant bubble. Starting 3 inches away, it penetrates the body about halfway through the abdomen, meaning that it will encompass your physical digestive organs but not the muscles and organs near the back of the body, such as the kidneys. The best way to find where the Spiritual Stomach ends in most people is to put your fingers on your sides at the level of the belly button, approximately midway between front and back. This is how far the Spiritual Stomach goes into the body.

- Allow yourself to feel or sense this bubble the best you can.
- At the front of this bubble will be the zipper. See or sense the bubble with the zipper at the front of it.

- You may not be able to sense your Spiritual Stomach the first time, or first several times, or you may just be aware of part of it. This is okay. Start from where you are. The Spiritual Stomach may not be a perfect bubble, it may present as a different shape. It also may be a color, a texture, or even a scent of some sort. Use as many senses as you can to get acquainted with this structure and its zipper.

When you can see or feel most of this structure (meaning the bubble and the zipper), you can continue:

- Allow yourself to feel or see the zipper mechanism again.
- Bring your physical hands to bring down the energetic zipper. When you do, allow yourself to temporarily unzip the zipper a few inches, or even fully to the bottom.
- As you do this, let your body know that you are now engaging your Spiritual Stomach, and that all the day's energy (from other people, from the environment, and other sources) that is not yours will now be taken care of by the spiritual instead of the physical digestive tract. As you say this, you may begin to feel an energy "poof" into the Spiritual Stomach, or you may feel your physical abdomen begin to distend a bit.

This practice takes a bit of work. To do it properly, it takes an understanding of the *Is This Mine?* exercise. After you have worked with it over a period of time, the Spiritual Stomach will begin regulating energy on its own, and "digesting" that which comes at us from our environment or from other people (what isn't ours) naturally. Eventually, the Spiritual Stomach will grow larger, and physical symptoms in the digestive tract are likely to dwindle (as long as physical reasons, such as diet, are also taken care of). As our capacity for understanding what is ours grows, we will find that our Spiritual Stomachs become much more effective at their job, and that our physical digestive tract is reserved for our own stressors, energies, and food intake.

Developing our Spiritual Stomachs allows us to digest energy in a very different manner. You may wish to work with the zipper mechanism, keeping it completely zipped up in places where you do not wish to take on any energy, such as in a bar or place where you are feeling uncomfortable. You may wish to keep it open and continually growing, eventually allowing yourself to be able to "digest" even the biggest energies around us, such as global, weather, astrological, and cosmic type events and energies. With practice, opening the Spiritual Stomach allows us to digest even the largest or most difficult of energies.

CHAPTER FIVE

Spiritual Hygiene

Maintaining a clear body and home, free from other influences, should be of the utmost importance to the psychic. Spiritual hygiene methods are ways to clear energies from in and around ourselves on a regular basis.

No matter how skilled we are, we tend to accumulate the energies of those around us in the course of our daily lives. This is especially true for people who work closely with others in the healthcare or customer service fields, but it can also be true for anyone, sensitive or not. We are in a sea of emotions, thoughts, spirits, and energies—some of them more difficult than others. We again return to the analogy of the nightlight, and how the more sensitive or psychic the person, the more brightly they tend to shine, attracting more stimuli into their fields or physical bodies.

The skills learned in the *Is This Mine?* meditation in the Basic Skills chapter can clear a wide variety of energies, but it is essential that you develop a regular spiritual hygiene routine for yourself and your home if you are to maintain clarity and release energies. It is only through regular spiritual clearing and cleansing that you can have clarity, peace of mind, and know how to properly release energies that may be having an impact on you.

A full spiritual hygiene routine includes spiritual bathing practices, clearing of the home or office, and personal care methods to get you through your day in between clearing sessions. All of these methods are safe, relatively simple, and when done over time can clear a huge amount of energy.

Cleansing practices can range from simple imagery for mild to moderate cleansing needs to a wide range of herbal, mineral, and other preparations that take several steps to do. Many of us understand how to use sage or salt or simple imagery such as white light to basically cleanse ourselves and our homes. While these methods are wonderful, especially when done on a regular basis (such as nightly self-Reiki practices), methods such as sage and visualizations of colored light are intended for milder situations, and many psychics find themselves without further tools to cleanse in more moderate or severe situations.

We have all sorts of energies around us and within us, and all of us, sensitive or not, will accumulate many different types of energies. Throughout our lives, and even in the course of a single day, we may experience a wide range of emotions, such as anger, pain, grief, and the various stresses of our day. We also experience our own thoughtforms—our thoughts have an energy all their own and project out into the world. We also experience physical reality—injuries in yoga class, running for the elevator at work, and the repetitive stress of sitting at our computer are all examples of the physical impact that is placed on our bodies on a daily basis. Beyond emotions, thoughtforms, stress, and our physical experiences of the world, we also all have a spiritual body and spiritual experiences that may or may not be in our conscious awareness. Whether we are conscious of our spiritual experiences or not, we have energy that stems from our spiritual selves that can be assisted by cleansing.

When we define ourselves, as in energy that is created by us, we are considering the physical body, meaning everything from our skin going inward. We are also talking about our energetic field, meaning the area that surrounds our physical bodies approximately 6-24 inches out, depending on the person. Our energy fields expand and contract quite a bit, depending on the situation we find ourselves in, how we are feeling, and the amount of emotional trauma we may have. As noted earlier, psychics, in particular, tend to shield and contract their energy as a subconscious coping mechanism.

Both the energy within and around us can be cleansed. In discussing energy that stems from our own experiences, emotions, and daily existence, it is important to understand that much of this energy will naturally dissipate—we are able to naturally process quite a bit of stimuli, especially if we are reasonably healthy. However, if we are under a great deal of stress, have physical illness or weakness, or have difficulty with our emotions, we will be unable to process all that happens to us in a day.

If, due to our personal history, we have a hard time expressing anger or other emotions, those emotions will linger in our physical bodies or energetic field. When we are physically, emotionally, mentally, and spiritually healthy, as well as willing to take personal responsibility for the emotions, stresses, thoughts, and other energies we create, we may find that we need to cleanse less than we once did.

Even when we take personal responsibility for our emotions, work through our stresses, let go of our thoughts, take care of ourselves physically, and are deeply in touch with our spiritual natures, we still may find ourselves overwhelmed by stimuli and in need of cleansing. This is due to our interactions and experiences with other humans, beings, and energies. Depending on how sensitive we are, we may notice that our neighbors fighting has an impact on our mood, that we get headaches and feel ill after being in traffic, or that we are anxious in a grocery store. When we check in with our feelings and ask "Is this mine?," the answer is a resounding "NO!"

This is because we are sensitive enough that the emotions, thought-forms, stresses, experiences, and even the physical ailments we come into contact with accumulate in our energy field as well as our physical bodies. So not only do we have the experiences and emotions from our own day, but those of the many people and environments we interact with, which are taken on by our energetic field and physical bodies. This is especially true for people who live in heavily populated areas, or in towns where there are a lot of heavy energies or events that have taken place. We may absorb this energy as an empath would, actually changing our energy to match what we come into contact with. We may also simply notice ourselves feeling drained, tired, or experiencing headaches, digestive issues, and other signs of feeling overwhelmed.

We may also notice, even if we are skilled at shielding, that these stimuli are accumulating and sitting on top of or just inside our seal or shield. The more we take into our physical body stimuli that do not stem from our-selves, and the deeper they penetrate, generally the more difficult it is to get rid of them.

If something is outside our bodies (such as in our energy field, or the space around us), and has simply accumulated, we may feel something there that is not ours, or know that we need to take basic self-care measures such as taking a nap, spending time in nature, or doing a yoga class or exercis-ing to reboot. When this energy comes into our field closer to our physi-cal bodies, we may feel it compressing us and feel closed in, anxious and overwhelmed. When energy enters our physical body, it is more likely to be physical, such as digestive issues and other pains.

Until we process not only our own emotions, stress, thoughts, and ex-periences but the stimuli coming at us from many different sources, we are likely to stay in a state of overwhelm and hypervigilance. By learning how to regularly spiritually cleanse, we can let go of our own experiences of this world and the energetic accumulations from our interactions with other people and situations. We will also be more able to use the tools already discussed, as well as begin to feel in control of our sensitivities and experiences in this world.

Spiritual Bathing

Ritualistic baths and cleansings with water have been around for as long as spiritual work has been documented. The spiritual properties and cleansing abilities of water have been documented through every major religion in the world—from the Torah to Biblical references to baths that bring Muslims closer to Allah. The power of water to clear, to heal, and to consecrate is evident in many of our modern-day religious ceremonies, such as baptisms.

There is a rich cultural and spiritual heritage that can be explored when it comes to water and simple baths intended to purify, cleanse, and support spiritual progress. American Indians, Russians, Celts, Druids, Indians, Africans, Egyptians, and pretty much any culture and nation has some sort of belief that water is an extension of divinity.

Water gives us life, and the energy of water allows us to clear what does not serve us in this world. Our bodies and our spiritual nature crave this connection to water, and our physical nature is primarily composed of water. Although this is not common knowledge, in our inner nature (our bodies), we have the same rhythms, tides, and waveforms that an ocean has. This inner ocean was our first experience of our world in utero, and the fluids of our bodies sustain us physically, energetically, and spiritually. The more we align ourselves with water energy, the more we are able to let go of energy that does not serve us, and the more we can feel spiritually nourished and connected.

In our modern day, we have lost our connection to the earth and the ceremonies and natural methods of clearing that we used to know. Even so, many psychics may find themselves drawn to water without knowing why, or notice that they want to take a shower or bath when they are feeling overwhelmed. Subconsciously, many of us may realize the clearing power of simply taking a shower. The simple power of water, alongside the proper intentions or prayers, can clear even the heaviest or most destructive of energies.

Although a powerful prayer or the power of your intent combined with water can clear a wide variety of energies, most of us do not have that capability. We do not come to spiritual bathing with the focus and power of intent that many spiritual practitioners cultivate over a period of decades, and those of us who are sensitive frequently come to spiritual bathing depleted,

MANAGING PSYCHIC ABILITIES

off balance, or simply in need of extra assistance. This is why a variety of minerals and herbs known for their clearing properties can be used to great effect. The herbs and other materials in the baths suggested below have spiritual and energetic properties of their own that increase the power and capabilities of a spiritual bath.

Unless we live by a stream, ocean, or body of water, many of us are somewhat removed from the healing power of natural sources of water. The healing power in the water that flows through the pipes in our homes is muted, and the power and its spiritual properties are diminished. If you do have a source of natural water nearby, I encourage you to gather some for spiritual bathing purposes. Even a tablespoon in your bathwater can allow you to feel the pure, divine connection more readily than a domestic water source. Using a simple bucket, you can also collect virgin rain water (water that has not fallen on the earth) and add it to your bath, increasing the natural potency of the Water element and your connection to it.

The health benefits of spiritual bathing are numerous. When we clear that which is not ours and old emotions and energies that are not serving us, we bring forth new vitality in our lives.

Spiritual bathing is used in different spiritual traditions for other reasons—from finding romance to increasing wealth to numerous physical health benefits. Spiritual bathing can be a complex art form with specific prescriptions for individual situations, and many spiritual practitioners have a deep understanding of the process. While the baths I describe below will clear a wide variety of energies, for exceptional cases, you may need to find a competent spiritual practitioner who can formally prescribe a spiritual bath specific to your situation.

If done on a regular basis, spiritual bathing can help us move forward in our lives, decrease spiritual stimuli around us, and feel more calm and relaxed. If we have never learned how to properly cleanse ourselves, it is likely that we have layers of energy surrounding and within us that are not our own. Over a period of time, spiritual bathing will remove these energies and allow us to move forward in our lives, along with the other tools already discussed.

How to Take a Spiritual Bath

Similar to how a shower or regular bath clears physical "grime," a spiritual bath is intended to clear spiritual "grime." But instead of removing physical dirt, a spiritual bath clears negative or blocking energies, vibrations, and emotions.

A spiritual bath should be done after regular physical bathing, as they are used for different purposes. The last thing we would want to do after a spiritual bath is to take a regular shower and dull the effects by adding regular shampoos, soaps, and body washes. In an ideal situation, a physical bath or shower will be taken, followed by a spiritual bath. If materials like salt are stuck in the hair, simply rinse afterwards with water. Otherwise, taking a spiritual bath in a reasonably physically clean state will suffice, and this will ensure that both physical and spiritual grime are cleared.

A spiritual bath once a week is suggested for anyone who is sensitive as a matter of routine. If major clearing is needed, I suggest you take three baths in a row, one each day. And for anyone having extreme difficulties with either energies or extreme negativity surrounding them or their home, I suggest taking seven baths in a row, one each day, or that you visit a spiritual practitioner familiar with spiritual bathing practices who can give individualized advice and instructions for your specific situation.

In some cases, people either do not have bathtubs or cannot take baths due to various medical issues. If you do not have a bathtub, put the ingredients in a bucket and sponge the mixture all over the body, from head to foot; you can also use the ingredients as a foot soak. The spiritual baths described in the following section all use a few simple ingredients combined with bath water. In most cases, you can simply gather the ingredients and put them in the bathtub.

If there are specific herbs or loose items, you can do the following:

- Get a cheesecloth, empty teabag, or coffee filter, insert the ingredients, and put them in the bath (tie it, if you need to, to stop the ingredients from spilling out).
- Get a bowl, put the ingredients in, make a sort of loose-leaf tea/decoction. Wait for it to infuse (turn dark—10 minutes or so), then strain the ingredients from the herbs, bringing the water portion to the bath with you.

This way the various herbs that you can use will not clog the tub, and it is much easier to clean up.

In a basic spiritual bath, you will put the ingredients in (or the tea mixture you have made), fill the rest of the tub with hot water, and get in. You will then take the bath water and gently pour it over the crown of your head, making passes either with a sponge or your hands down your body (from head to feet, not forgetting the arms), stating that anything that is not yours can clear. Since people often like specific numbers, I suggest doing a pass either three or nine times, both numbers that are appropriate for clearing. On the last pass down your body, you will stand up in the bath and unplug the drain so that the "dirty" water (the water with the negativity and energies you have just cleared) can go down the drain.

While you are filling the tub, you will state your prayers or intents, and as you are clearing yourself (bringing the mixture from top to bottom of your body) you will also pray, ask for clearing, or call on whatever feels right to you to clear. Since prayer is specific to your individual spiritual path, traditions, and your own convictions, it is best to use a prayer or simple intent in line with your own faith rather than take from a tradition that is not your own or that you may not personally believe in. For example, taking a psalm from the Bible, if it is not your path, is not very effective, but creating a specific focused intent and praying from your heart is.

Some people choose to light a white candle and place it outside the tub for when they get out, signifying purity and a fresh start; or they may light two candles and step between them upon exiting the tub, as a sign that they are entering into a cleared space. Others may choose to light incense specific to their purposes and clear their home prior to getting into their spiritual bath, or they may place specific items around the bathtub, such as crystals or gemstones. However you decide to work with lit items, such as candles, basic precautions and considerations for your safety apply, and you should keep anything lit within eyesight so you know what is going on with anything burning.

A spiritual bath is not intended to be a lengthy thing, 5-20 minutes is fine. People who are more sensitive may feel a lot of release, and others may need to take a few baths to notice changes in their energy or mood. After your bath you will then get out of the tub, dry with a fresh towel, dress in fresh clothes, and go about your day.

BATH: Simple Steps to a Spiritual Bath

- Gather your ingredients.
- Bring them to the bathtub.
  - If you are using loose herbs, either put them in a cheesecloth or make a tea out of them, bringing the "tea" portion to the tub with you.
- Put the ingredients in the bath, and add water.

- (Optional) light a candle, incense, or arrange other items such as crystals.
- Get in the bathtub and soak.
- Make downward passes of the bath water, from top to bottom of your body.
- State prayers or intents for energies not serving you to clear.
- On the last pass, stand up in the bathtub, and pull the plug on your drain.
- Get out of the tub, blow out the candle, dry with a fresh towel, and gather any remainder bath ingredients from the tub to throw away.
- Get dressed in fresh, clean clothes, and put the shower on briefly to clear any residue from the bathtub.

This is the simplest way to do a spiritual bath, and although it seems like a lot of steps, it becomes quite simple once it is done a few times. As mentioned, spiritual bathing is spiritual art, meaning that there are a variety of rituals, uses for spiritual herbs, and prayers that can be involved. But all of the baths we will go over will clear a lot of energy from a variety of sources and are highly effective in their simplicity.

Sensory Deprivation Tank

As long as the psychic is not claustrophobic, a sensory deprivation tank is an incredibly useful method of spiritual bathing with no setup required. This method has the added benefit of blocking out sound and light (if this is chosen by the person while entering the tank). It allows the experiencer to process and cleanse themselves of many lingering energies in and around them, due to the high mineral content and the ability to "float" without having to negotiate with gravity.

Taking a Shower

One of the easiest methods of cleansing is to take a simple shower. After each day of working or going out into the world, especially if you have had considerable stress or are feeling overwhelmed, getting in the shower with the intention that you will "wash away the day" will be extraordinarily helpful in clearing away accumulated energies. Some people with the appropriate training will do Reiki symbols into their showerhead, or will imagine white light emanating from their shower. Most of us will notice, with or without any intentions, that we feel better after taking a shower. In the shower, a cheesecloth or similar item can be used with a drop or two of essential oils on it, then tied around your showerhead with a rubber band or other mechanism to create a simple, effective way to clear. Suggested essential oils include lemon, pine, or eucalyptus, both for their smell and clearing abilities. Essential oils are powerful, so you do not want to drench the cloth with them—a drop or two is more than enough. Also make sure that whatever you are using to put essential oils on is porous enough so that water from your showerhead gets through, otherwise you may find yourself with a huge mess.

Many different salt scrubs and body scrubs on the market contain a variety of clearing herbs, such as rosemary, citrus, and tea tree oil. While not a substitute for a full spiritual bath, these methods can be used quickly and simply when you either do not have time for a full spiritual bath, or in between maintenance baths. If you are feeling really overwhelmed or in need of major cleansing, simply taking a shower will help but a full spiritual bath will be much more effective.

BATH: Goat's Milk and Parsley Bath

Goat's milk is available at a variety of retailers and is a gentle, well-known clearer of energy. Parsley is an herb that focuses on clearing, and its usage in different spiritual traditions includes everything from clearing evil spirits to protection to stopping nightmares to simply having a stress relief and calming effect on your spirit.

This is a bath that will gently release many different energies from in and around you. You can simply get some goat's milk and put the parsley directly in the container, allowing it to infuse for a number of hours, and then put 2-4 cups of it into the bath, filling the rest up with hot water and then getting in. You may also wish to gently heat the goat's milk with the parsley on the stovetop, then bring it to the bathtub.

It is important to allow the parsley to infuse properly to work with its spiritual properties. If you are looking for simplicity, you are welcome to put the goat's milk and parsley directly in your bathtub and simply wait 10-20 minutes for it to infuse and then add hot water. If you put parsley straight in the bathtub, I do suggest putting the parsley in a cheesecloth or small bag, so that cleanup after the bath is not difficult and the herbs do not clog your drain. As noted earlier, you will simply get in the bathtub and bring some of the mixture from the top of your body to the bottom, simply asking for any energy in or around you to leave. If you follow a specific spiritual path or faith, you may also include appropriate prayers from that faith. If there was a specific intent for the bath, such as releasing emotions, you are welcome to add your specific concern. On the last pass you will stand up in the tub and allow the water to drain.

Even with difficult energies, a regular routine of once a week or so of the goat's milk and parsley bath will allow most people to feel much clearer in a few weeks.

BATH: Salt, Lemon, and Bay Leaf Bath

Similar to our other spiritual baths, a salt, lemon, and bay leaf bath is a simple way to clear a variety of energies from in and around you. This bath requires between ½ cup and 2 cups of salt (either Epsom salts, kosher, or sea salt), half a lemon, and a bay leaf. All members of the citrus family are powerful energy clearers, and lemon is especially uplifting in the way it releases energy. Salt has an ability to drain energy from you as well as be relaxing and stress-reducing, and bay leaf is known for its ability to combat and keep away negative energies. Similar to the other baths, you may wish to put the half of a lemon and bay leaf in a bag for easy cleanup purposes after your bath.

It should be noted that due to its energetic draining and opening nature, some people are too sensitive or porous for salt. What this means is that you will be feeling really drained and too "open" after this type of bath. It is typical for senses and psychic abilities to heighten and get clearer after a spiritual bath, but for some, the amount of material coming at them, combined with the energetic nature of the salt, results in feelings of being overwhelmed, tired, and like there is too much stimuli coming at you. If this happens, the easiest thing to do is to cut down on the amount of salt, such as using 2 tablespoons of salt instead of 2 cups. If you find that you are still feeling drained after a salt bath, the goat's milk bath is a good alternative.

BATH: Coffee and Salt Bath

A slightly more intense clearing bath is a coffee and salt bath. Pouring a cup of coffee with 1-2 cups of salt in the bathtub can release a wide variety of energies, including spirit attachments. The brand or type of coffee does not seem to matter, and even a few teabags of instant coffee for those who do not have coffee in the house is effective. If teabags are used, give them 10 minutes or so to create a tea in your bathtub for you to soak in.

Most bathtubs in relatively modern houses are fairly stainproof, but some do stain if you use darker substances such as coffee. If you are not sure if your bathtub will stain, do a test patch first before dumping a cup of coffee in it.

BATH: Cascarilla, Camphor, Florida Water, and Holy Water (or Rain Water) Bath

Most of the time, simplicity is best—a simple coffee and salt bath can clear an incredible amount of energy. We are likely to find over time that a regular practice of a spiritual bathing will clear even the densest or most difficult of energies. But in certain cases, where someone may be feeling a lot of intense negativity around them, a major blockage in their life, or that they desperately need something to change in their lives, this bath can provide clearing and opening.

Sometimes we need a "blast" approach to clearing, which this bath does. Although it is probably much stronger than anyone actually needs, it is one of my favorites for clearing pretty much anything that may be in or around you. It is a modern formulation, meaning that it uses herbs from a variety of cultures and spiritual traditions, while the other baths are from a specific culture or more traditional in their approach.

A lot of psychics are in the helping professions, working as massage therapists, counselors, and medical professionals, and it is natural for people in these professions to take on energy from their clients, especially if they are unskilled. But even with a lot of skill, people seeking help may have energies attached to them that unknowingly (or knowingly) move over to the psychic. Most competent spiritual workers have a spiritual bathing practice in order to clear themselves of energy, especially after a hard day, and will be strict about energetic hygiene practices in order to keep themselves clear, safe, and in good health.

Cascarilla is powdered egg shells, and although this can be made at home, it is cheaply sold in botanicas, spiritual stores, some new age—type stores, as well as online. Camphor is typically sold in squares, and either powdering or crushing a square or two to put in the bathtub with a teaspoon of cascarilla will create a powerful clearing combination.

Holy Water is well known for its powerful clearing abilities, but if you are not affiliated with a church or do not have a faith supporting the use of Holy Water, rain water or natural water from a stream or body of water near you is a wonderful substitute. A tablespoon of Holy Water or 2 cups or so of natural water is needed for this bath.

Florida water has become popular recently, with many different people making formulations of different herbs and calling it by the name "Florida water." This can be difficult for the consumer, as many of the people creating Florida water may not know how to work with herbs, or may have a recipe that is not as effective as others. Unless you know and have confidence in a local herbalist, I suggest you look for Murray & Lanman's version of Florida water, as they were the original formulators and still have a strong presence in many spiritual markets. A simple capful or a few splashes of Florida water in the bath is enough for this specific bath.

In looking at these spiritual baths, it is important to choose one that resonates with you. It is in our nature to gravitate towards the strongest spiritual bath, but it is actually more important to try these baths out and see which one you individually seem to work best with. For most people a simple spiritual bath once a week will suffice, with perhaps the shower methods discussed in between. For those in the healing and caring professions, I suggest a weekly spiritual bath plus one any time you may feel "off" or like you have perhaps taken on energy from your work place, clients, or the people surrounding you.

Clearing and Cleansing Your Home

There are two basic steps in maintaining a regular energetic hygiene routine: clearing yourself (spiritual bathing), and clearing your home. If both are done on a regular basis, such as once a week, the results are often palpable.

Our home is intended to be a safe place, which is an important concept for psychics. We are so used to being assaulted by stimuli that a place of peace, quiet, and solitude is necessary for us to not go into a space of overload. Our home may not be a safe place, though—it may, in fact, be a place of energetic accumulation. We may have gotten into arguments with our partner or roommates, have neighbors that have difficult energy, or have had people live in our space prior to us that brought negativity in. We may also have spirits in our homes or spirits and other energies may be attracted to us because of our sensitivity level.

Again we return to the analogy of the nightlight, and how the more sensitive we are the more brightly our nightlight shines. This allows us to be aware of more of what is around us, but also for what is around us to be aware of us. So spirits seeking our help, energies that are simply curious, and spiritual and energetic occurrences that may not happen to others who are less sensitive (either because of this sort of nightlight and magnetizing effect, or they simply would not notice) happen more regularly to psychics.

As discussed earlier, we are also in a sea of thoughts and emotions—our own as well as of those around us. If we do not clear our space, we allow these energies to accumulate, eventually creating energetic congestion and blocking the proper exchange of energies. We often have layers and layers of energies piled on top of us—simply from being sensitive and trying to go about our daily lives. With proper cleansing, we can begin to remove those layers and feel more at peace in our homes as well as our bodies.

There are a lot of good herbs, minerals, and products for cleansing the home. By properly learning how to use them, we can create the right amount of clearing for our home and its needs.

Cleansing Ingredients

When those of us in mainstream spiritual communities think of clearing, inevitably using sage to clear homes and people comes up. The method for using sage as a clearing agent is well known: simply light the sage and allow the smoke to waft or be fanned into the corners of the home (or wherever we may be cleansing), as well as fanned or blown over ourselves. This method can clear both our energy fields as well as our homes of a significant portion of energetic accumulation, mainly lingering thoughts, emotions, and experiences that were brought into our homes or energy fields.

Sage's popularity is interesting, considering that its main spiritual property is actually consecration, basically the dedication of a space for spiritual rituals and ceremonies. The fact that it clears is almost a secondary function—the clearing effect, especially when it is used solo (meaning not with other herbs such as tobacco or sweetgrass) is fairly minimal, and limited to mild and moderate clearing purposes.

For sage, or any plant or mineral, to be effective we both need to resonate with the plant and honor it. It is best to bless the sage, or have it blessed by someone who is knowledgeable on how to do so. While all herbs and minerals have innate spiritual functions, it is in the blessing, our personal focus, and our gratitude for the herb or mineral that it truly has its own spirit and functions on a much more powerful level. We may also find that we have allergies to specific scents, or work in an office where there are clients or others who are sensitive to particular scents. Using essential oils, or products such as cascarilla, Florida water, lemon-based products, or pine for cleansing, is less likely to cause irritation to you, your clients, or any guests you have in your home. Proper ventilation after using some of these methods, such as opening windows, is also helpful so that heavy energies have an exit, as well as scents become less dominant in the space.

We may use sage because it is what we know how to do, but because of our personal history, sensate experience, as well as other factors we may find that sage is not the correct basic clearer for us. Instead, we may find that we resonate more with other basic cleansing methods, such as lemon, pine, copal, salt, or palo santo instead. Depending on the area in which we live, we may also consider that local ingredients, or herbs and minerals that are native to our region, are more effective or we resonate with them on a deeper level.

Lemon (or really any citrus) is a good, basic cleanser, as noted earlier. It will clear out a great deal of accumulated energy and is easy to find in most grocery stores. Buy an empty spray bottle and a lemon, cut the lemon in half and squeeze the lemon juice into the spray bottle. Fill up the rest of the bottle with purified, distilled, rain, or comparable water. Let this sit for a few hours or a day or two in the refrigerator. If you have carpets, simply spray a fine mist into the air and on the carpets. Similar to other herbal methods, you can say your intent (such as wanting to cleanse and remove any negative energy). You can also spray yourself with lemon water, but make sure to not get any in your eyes. If you are doing wash water (water in a bucket for floors), you can simply go about cleaning the floors of your house, first doing a test patch first to ensure that you are not going to strip any hardwood or discolor any tile floors with the water.

Many of us are familiar with Pine Sol, a widely available cleaning product. Some may be surprised that pine is a powerful, effective energetic cleanser as well. Original Pine Sol (check to make sure it has actual pine in it), pine essential oils, or simply gathering pine needles and creating a tea out of them are all extremely effective at not only cleansing emotions and accumulated energy but also negative energies, such as beings and spirits. As with lemon, Original Pine Sol or pine essential oils can be put with water to wash or in a spray bottle to cleanse the home. If gathering pine needles you simply want to remove the base of the needles (the part that looks like paper and is typically brown) and chop up the needles. You will then boil water on your stovetop and put the pine needles in it, then turn off the heat, put a lid on the pan, and allow the needles to steep. Use the pine water as a spray or floor wash. Most people prefer to drain the needles out using cheesecloth, a strainer, or other methods so that there isn't a big mess of random needles around the house.

Copal is an incense resin that is typically gathered from Mexico and Central America. Copal comes in both black and white forms. Black copal naturally oozes from the copal tree. White copal resin is gathered by scraping the trees or putting marks in the tree, similar to tapping for maple syrup. Copal is very effective at spiritual cleansing, particularly in cases of spiritual illness, or spirits or energies affecting the physical body.

Copal is considered an important herb because it not only clears thoughts, emotions, and energies but also spirits and beings. This also makes it more effective in more moderate to severe cases of energetic accumulation. Copal is typically burned on a charcoal disk. Packs of charcoal are widely available in most new age and occult shops. Since copal is a sticky resin the coal will be lit, thus releasing the natural properties of the incense on top of it. To do this, you will need an incense pot or fireproof bowl with sand in it. You will then use a long pair of tweezers or pair of tongs to hold the charcoal disk and light it. Once it is lit, put it in the sand or incense pot and place the resin on top. Some charcoal disks have a small divot into which you can place the resin; this will allow air to circulate properly so that the resin begins to smoke. You then go through your space and, as you would when using sage, ensure that you get some of the smoke into the corners of the rooms as well as throughout the room.

Salt is both easily accessible and an effective mild to moderate cleanser. You can use any kind of salt for cleansing, although kosher and sea salt are typical. For cleansing purposes, salt can be placed in the corners of a room (just a pinch) as well as in the center of the room. Some of us may find we need to do this in each room, especially if there is a felt sense of something "off" about a particular room. We may also find it necessary to put a pinch of salt in each of the outside corners of our home (do this both on the inside of your house, as well as the outside). In more severe situations, a perimeter of salt around the house, on window ledges, or in the doorway of a particular room may be needed to keep energies at bay.

Palo santo, also known as "Holy Wood," comes from South America. It is a moderate cleanser, well known for energetically cleansing, as well as clearing even the heaviest of emotions and thoughts and physical ailments. It additionally is an opener, meaning that it not only cleanses but allows us to see, feel, or sense more of what is around us spiritually. It typically comes as a small piece of wood (although you can get this as a ready-made oil as well) that you simply light and use, similar to how you would burn sage.

Cascarilla, already covered in the Spiritual Bathing section, is powdered egg shells and is used in house clearing in the same way that salt is, by putting some in the corners of the house or the room you wish to clear. It is generally considered to be very clearing, and is used to keep away negative spirits and purify any space it is placed in.

Like copal, dragon's blood is a resin that is placed upon a charcoal disk for use in clearing. It is highly clearing for spaces that have significant energetic issues. Unlike other products, dragon's blood should be purchased in the resin form only—the essential oils on the market frequently do not contain the resin (and will have red food coloring instead) or will contain a very small amount of the resin.

Traditionally, herbs like myrrh (clears heavy emotions and other energies), cedar (chips, oil, or even pieces of the wood), frankincense (clears and brings peace), bay leaves (clears evil and negativity), parsley (clears negativity), and basil (drives away evil) are herbs that are frequently used to clear spaces. Other more caustic substances such as ammonia, and products like camphor squares already suggested in the Spiritual Bathing section are also heavily used for clearing the home of significant negativity.

It is easy to feel overwhelmed by the number of choices one has for clearing and cleansing the home. But in most cases, home cleansing is fairly simple. An herb or product that can be lit or smoked, plus a "wash" (herbs in water in a spray bottle or bucket) are all you really need.

How to Cleanse Your Home

Cleansing the home is traditionally done top to bottom, back to front. This means that if you live in a house that is more than one story, you should start cleansing on the top floor of your house and work downward, floor by floor, moving to the ground floor, the basement (if there is one), and ending at the front door. A regular cleansing routine, such as once a week, is typically suggested. If you are unable to cleanse the entire house or apartment in one day, you would still use the top to bottom, back to front method, but would do a thorough cleanse of the designated room(s). Then when you wish to carry on with the rest of your house on another day, you would go through the already cleansed rooms, doing a simple walk-through with your lit item (such as palo santo, or dragon's blood) before beginning in the next room that needs clearing.

The first step in any home cleansing is to physically clear the space. This means putting things away. It is especially important for highly sensitive psychics to have a living space that does not have a lot of items lying around, as this just means we have more stimuli to process. Once the house is physically cleared, you can prepare your ingredients if you have not done so already. For a thorough cleansing, you will need to use a cleansing ingredient for the floor as well as one that can be burned and fill the air. For a very basic cleansing, I suggest using lemon water and salt. Buy an empty container, fill it with the ingredients, and allow it to sit for a while. Some people choose to add a bay leaf or basil to this mixture, if they feel there is significant negative energy to clear out.

You would then choose an item to clear the air that can be lit, such as palo santo, copal, or dragon's blood. Some of the other herbs mentioned, such as cedar, myrrh, frankincense, or pine needles, can also be placed upon charcoal disks and used in a similar way. It is important to choose herbs, minerals, or other products that you personally resonate with and have the spiritual properties you are looking for.

Go to the first room, close the window, and allow smoke to fill the room. Some people choose to buy a feather or some sort of tool to waft the smoke through the room; others will simply bring the product to the four corners of the room, ensuring that it fills the room with its essence. As you work with any of these ingredients it is best to thank them for their service and to state your intent (such as "I wish to clear my home of negativity") as you are using them. If you are unable to light anything in your space, essential oils can be used in very small amounts, or the spray bottle of lemon-salt water can simply be used more often.

As with any item that you are burning for cleansing purposes, you will want to extinguish it completely and put it in a safe place to make sure that you do not set a fire in your home after you have finished clearing it.

You will then use your spray bottle mixture on the carpeting, or wash the floors with lemon water. Again, do a test patch with any mixture you decide to use, to make sure it does not harm your floors or furniture. You may also choose to spray down the windows and walls, although this is often not necessary.

End by putting a pinch of salt in each of the corners of the room, as well as the center of the room. If you are having more significant energetic issues, you may choose to put a camphor square or sprinkle some cascarilla in the corners of each room. If there are pets or small children that occupy your space, place the camphor square in a glass of water above where the child can reach. For full clearing purposes, you may choose to "five spot" or put a dab of the wash water on the corners of each windowpane and the center, both inside and out, again stating your intent of keeping any energies at bay.

After you have smoked the room, open the window to allow all energies an easy way to leave. You may then choose to imagine white light flowing through the room, or place a small white candle in the room and light it (making sure it is safe and won't light anything on fire) before you leave.

Go from room to room, using the same methods of clearing. When you get to your front door, walk outside and place a pinch of salt in each of the outside corners of the house and do a "five spot" on your front door. If you are having significant difficulties and would like to protect your home, red brick dust (which is powdered red bricks and has a protection function) can be placed in a line under your doormat in order to keep negative energies at bay. Finally, dispose of the remnants of your sage and lemon water off your property.

When you return, again go through the house, from top to bottom, back to front, closing the windows and blowing out or snuffing the lit candles. After all the windows are closed and the candles are out, replace the salt water bowl or bowls in the room of your choosing (we will discuss this further in the Personal Care Methods section). Continue to do personal cleansing methods, such as spiritual bathing. A simple method of creating wash water is to choose your spiritual bath ingredients and use some of the bath water for house cleansing (again ensuring that you are not using a product that will stain carpets or furniture) and then after house cleansing take a spiritual bath.

This is a very basic method of cleansing. A typical physical cleansing and clearing schedule (to get rid of dust, dirt, and grime) might involve first putting away items, then dusting and vacuuming and using regular cleaning methods, then spiritually cleansing each room. If you live with roommates, see if they are open-minded about you cleansing your room as well as common areas. If you are in an apartment, you can still cleanse your whole apartment and dispose of the remnants of your cleansing solution off your property. You can also put salt at the corners of your property, even if you are on a second floor of the apartment building. If you are living in a situation where you are only able to cleanse your own room, it is suggested that you do it more often.

Working with individual ingredients can get overwhelming for the psychic new to house clearing, so expect some trial and error at first. We all resonate with and are interested in different products. This is due to our backgrounds, culture, religion, and just personal taste as far as scent.

Although certainly I would use herbs like palo santo, dragon's blood, or copal in heavier cleansing situations, I may also use palo santo more often because I like the smell. Since you will be cleansing on a regular basis, and have to live with the scents in your home, as well as the energy created or cleared by these methods, you may prefer to use different cleansing ingredients—for example, pine water, because you enjoy the smell and perhaps sense evil or negative presences.

After trying basic clearers, such as sage or lemon water, we may find that they did not clear much and want to use something more powerful. It's natural to reach for heavier-duty herbs known for "blasting" energy out of the home when, in fact, ingredients with moderate clearing properties and that bring in feelings of lightness (such as lemon water) may be more appropriate. Some house clearing situations require heavier clearing agents, but in most cases, spritzing more often with a spray bottle of lemon and salt water solution may be more beneficial.

By working with herbs and minerals on a spiritual level, we begin to have relationships with them. We can choose to become spiritual allies with them, to meditate with or on their properties, and to thank them for helping us cleanse. It is a good basic practice to begin thanking the tools, the herbs and minerals, and the energies we use. When we develop a relationship on a deeper level (by even saying a simple thank you to the sage that we were using, for example), we will find over time that these methods work faster and are more effective. So each time you use a herb or other ingredient, say a simple thank you before and after you cleanse with it.

After cleansing your home it should feel lighter, more peaceful, and your mind should become quieter. If your home does not feel "cleared," or you still sense a presence, an energy that isn't yours, or even a worsening of emotions or energies, you will need to use more advanced methods. In certain negative environments, you might feel a temporary worsening of the energy the day afterward, in response to clearing. This is because energies and spirits are clearing from your home. This is a sign that clearing needs to be carried out more often, or needs to be done several days in a row.

In most cases, the herbs and methods listed in the previous sections on Spiritual Cleansing will work—it just takes some time. If you are dealing with an intense level of spirit involvement, difficult emotions, heavy imprints (something traumatic happened in the past at the location), or a house has such feelings of an uncomfortable nature that other cleansing methods either do not work or only work for short periods of time, you may have to cleanse a room on a regular basis, gradually clearing out the energies there.

Our homes did not get energetically congested in a day, and we should not expect them to clear with one house cleansing. If the house you are in is heavily congested, a weekly process of clearing the home and spiritual bathing will begin to show effects in a few short weeks. If there is something difficult, dangerous, or negative going on in the home, clearing a room where you sense this activity nine days in a row is often necessary, as noted earlier.

Sometimes with intense negativity (and not just energetic accumulation that will take some time to clear), it is best to call in a spiritual worker who can cleanse the home for you, or who can tell you the best methods or products to use in clearing your home. Proper spiritual workers will do a divination of the home, and will tell you what is going on, rather than doing a general cleansing with sage. They will then take appropriate action for your space and individual case. A good spiritual worker can talk with the energies of the home, the land you are on, and work with them to come to a state of balance.

In order to maintain ongoing energetic hygiene and a clear space in your home, many of the Personal Care practices discussed in the next section are helpful. You may choose to keep the spray bottle of ingredients you have created and do touch-ups in your home throughout the week, as well as use the salt and citrus bowl.

Plants are known for not only creating a sense of peace but as energetic space clearers. This is why in difficult or negative energetic situations, plants typically die or stop thriving. But there are some plants that can either be around the outside of the home or brought inside that are particularly known for their ability to clear, such as cacti, rosemary bushes (especially known for helping women and children), or the common household plant known as either snake plant or Saint George's sword. These plants not only clear the environment but their ability to thrive in your home serves as a warning of any problems there that you should be aware of.

Personal Care

The following simple practices can be used in your home, office, or on the go to maintain spiritual hygiene in between regular spiritual bathing and home clearing practices. They are useful in real world situations, at home, in the work place, or interacting with people in our daily lives, in addition to a regular spiritual hygiene routine, and can help us participate more fully and healthfully in the world.

CLEANSING: White Light Method

This is a method of clearing mild and relatively simple occurrences of energetic accumulation. However, although it is for mild situations, this does not mean that it is less important as a clearing method. When we ignore mild situations or energetic accumulations for periods of time they grow and become more difficult to deal with. By having a basic, daily cleansing routine we are less likely to need moderate or significant cleansing.

One of my favorite methods of basic clearing is using white light, or divine light. This is a favorite method because it is simple, effective, and can be done within a very short span of time. Pick one or two times each day (either morning or evening) to use this method. People who are trained in Reiki can certainly use Reiki self-care methods in place of this, but others of us (even if we are trained in Reiki) prefer this simpler yet powerful version of working with light.

You are welcome to sit or lie down to do this, and you may choose to open if you wish.

When you are ready, you are simply going to invite white light (or divine light) into your body. Feel it go through your whole body and allow it to surround and flow through you. Some of us may wish to feel this like a waterfall going through the crown down. Others may wish to have white light come through our whole field into our bodies. Feel it flow into every cell, every organ, and every part of your body. Ask it to clear anything negative, anything that is not yours, and any stress or emotions that may have accumulated. When you feel a sense of peace and relaxation you are done. You may wish to say "thank you" or just go about the rest of your day or evening. If you work with a specific concept of the divine, such as god, goddess, specific deity, angel, or other presence, you may wish to have them facilitate this light. If you do not, or do not wish to even consider anything "divine," you can simply work with the imagery of white light and imagine it clearing accumulated energy.

This method can be used in pretty much any situation, but is best when done on a regular basis, even if it is only for a few minutes a day. Since the white light method is a "mild" method of clearing, the effects are cumulative, meaning that if you do it once a day it is much more clearing that only doing it once a week or a month. This method is also suggested just before or right after a stressful experience, such as driving, speeches, board meeting, school exams, and more.

In time, you may notice that when you sit with this light it emanates from the inside out (rather than feeling it coming from the outside in). This is entirely natural, and when it occurs, allowing yourself to feel it emanate through the midline (your spinal column) outward can be a simple method of clearing that can be done quickly and effectively.

CLEANSING: Salt or Citrus Bowl

The Salt Bowl method is one of the easiest ways to maintain a cleansed home. Designate a specific bowl or two for this method. Once you do this you will only use this bowl for cleansing purposes as it will be collecting energies that are heavy or negative in nature. You will put salt (kosher or sea salt) and then water into a bowl. If you wish you can also put white light into the bowl as well through holding the bowl of salt water while you do the white light method. After you put salt and then water into the bowl, you will simply leave it out in the room or rooms of your choice. Replace the contents daily. You can do so by dumping the salt water down the toilet and then refilling the bowl with salt and water. Although this method seems deceptively simple, salt water is very effective at clearing thoughts, emotions, and other energies from a home.

Similarly, a bowl with citrus peels can be set out for similar energetic purposes. This method has the benefit of smelling wonderful as well as clearing your home. Although this is common sense, the citrus peels will need to be disposed of in the trash rather than down the drain or toilet.

Although a salt bowl or citrus bowl will naturally pick up energies in your home or office, energy can be directed to this bowl through breath. This is done by you feeling whatever stress, emotion, or energetic accumulation you may pick up and imagining yourself blowing it out of your mouth into the salt bowl. You do not need to be near the salt bowl to do this, but being in the same room is helpful.

CLEANSING: Washing Your Hands

Another method of basic cleansing is hand washing. This is a wonderful method for when you are on the go or in situations like restaurants and meetings. It can involve simply washing your hands or placing your hands under running water with the intent that any accumulated energy flow down the drain. This method especially works for feelings of overwhelm associated with social situations, or if you may be in a situation, such as a bar or restaurant, that has a lot of energies that are affecting you.

To do this method in an advanced way, feel the energetic accumulation you have picked up in or around you and visualize it as a color. Now put your hands under running water and intend as well as visualize that color draining out of you and into the running water and down the drain. Although this is another deceptively simple method, it can instantaneously cut down on feelings of overwhelm, anxiety, and stress associated with interacting with environments that may have too much stimuli, or that we are unable to properly process through other tools at the time.

Calibrating Energy

A simple calibration can be done by psychics in social situations to assess and take personal responsibility for what they are experiencing. This is a simple tool that is likely to make more sense after you have worked with boundaries and protections.

Many psychics find that they have a long-standing pattern of being called "too sensitive," which has caused them to feel out of place in this world. They also may find that when they interact with people, they get accused of similarly being too sensitive or taking offense in situations where another person does not mean to offend them. While it is understandable to have a variety of experiences in this world in which you are an outlier, or too sensitive to fit into this world, part of what happens when we interact with others is that we may be, in fact, being too sensitive.

This is a hard thing to accept. Psychics are able to more readily see the subtext of the world around them. We may notice underlying emotions, thoughts, biases, beliefs, and other information coming from other people when interacting with them. If we do not understand that this is something that we are simply picking up, rather than something that is directed at us, we may believe that people are angry or otherwise directing energy toward us that they did not intend to.

This means that even if the person we are speaking with is stating something reasonable, we may be picking up that the person is angry. The unskilled psychic will assume that the anger being displayed is part of the conversation, or may even think that the anger is directed toward them. Meanwhile, the person the psychic is speaking with may be unaware that they are showing anything other than the surface-level conversation pleas-antness they are intending.

Although it can be difficult to sense an inner truth of someone with whom we are speaking, that subtext, emotions, experiences, or whatever else we may be picking up from someone is not a part of their conscious reality, and is not intended to be an aspect of the relationship or conversation. Recognition that this pattern may be happening in our social interactions with others is a good first step in working with this pattern. We can also do a simple calibration of our energy in social situations so we can properly assess and clearly understand what is, in fact, occurring.

It is only recently with certain television shows that psychics of all sorts go up to people in supermarkets and in daily life and announce that they have a spirit with them, or that they can sense something about them. Ethically, we are only intended to have as much information about someone as they provide us, and we are all mistaken in what we pick up at times. Even if someone has a big sign above their head in neon lights saying "CANCER," it is not our duty or responsibility to tell them, and in fact is ethically wrong to do so. We all have secrets, emotions, and traumas that we likely do not wish the world to find out.

Unless that person is specifically going to a psychic in a professional capacity, it is generally best practice to keep our mouths shut about what we sense, see, or feel about the person we are conversing with. It is often the case that those who go up to people and state that they can see, sense, or hear beyond ordinary capacity are doing it not out of an altruistic intent but because they wish to intrude energetically on other people or escape their own inner work.

Although talk of ethics can be a bit difficult when it comes to sensitivities and psychic abilities, it is important to keep it in mind when discussing social interactions as well as the basic tool of calibration.

As psychics we naturally calibrate, or change, our energy to meet the energetic environment of the room or the people in it. We may do this in some ways more than others, and people with empathic tendencies and people who are highly sensitive tend to do this more than others. Although this is again a seemingly simple practice, it takes a bit of practice to do well.

EXERCISE: Calibrating Energy

- First, you will pick someone out in the room. This may be someone you are conversing with.
- You will now do a basic assessment of their emotion. What is their dominant emotion? It may be sadness, anger, grief, despair, or even a frozen state.
- Now consider what the energy is of that person. Do this on a very basic level. Do they seem lively and full of energy? Or depleted, sick, or lacking energy?
- Now consider the energy dynamics of the person. When they interact with others, are they taking energy? Or are they bringing energy? When they walk into a room, does the room brighten and seem full of cheer? Or does it seem gloomier or darker with them in it?
- Now that you have noticed the above information, look at their mask. Their mask is how they wish to present themselves to the world. This may change a bit from person to person, but most people put on a specific mask in social situations. This person may be unmasked a bit if they are drinking or using drugs, but overall you should be able to consider this information.
- Now realize that their emotion, energy, and energetic dynamics are things that they may not want you to see or sense.

When we learn to separate what is on the surface (the mask) from what we are noticing (what lies underneath), we naturally begin to react to people differently. We no longer get offended (or not as much), because we realize that our interactions with people are rarely about us. Each person is in their own private world of emotion and energy dynamics, and is likely struggling with that information as well as putting on a proper mask to the world. When we realize this we can begin to have more compassion for people. We can also realize that how people interact with us is often not about us, to not take things personally, and to begin to interact, or calibrate our energy differently around them.

This will naturally happen through discovering their dominant emotion and energy; there is nothing further that we need to do. The more we go through this sort of checklist (emotion, energy, dynamics, mask), the more we will naturally begin to react differently to the person.

When we do this properly, we will begin to realize that the person we are speaking with is intending to speak to us in a polite way, and we are just sensing their anger and other issues. We can then realize that their issues are their own and not react to them; instead, we simply respond to the mask they are presenting, or excuse ourselves from speaking to them in the first place, if we have determined that the person is angry and sucking energy out of everyone in the room.

CHAPTER SIX

Developing Boundaries
and Protections

In addition to the skills and understandings already discussed, developing boundaries and protections is an often neglected or misunderstood skill needed by all psychics who wish to function in a healthy way in the world.

It is typical for the sensitive or psychic to either have really rigid boundaries or to have no energetic boundaries at all. It is important to know which category you are in (or if you are in both categories), in order to begin to take personal responsibility for your energetic body as well as alleviate the symptoms associated with having too rigid or too expanded boundaries.

When we are unskilled as psychics, we tend to retract and protect ourselves from oncoming stimuli. Many times this is an unconscious sort of protection, and we will notice in our physical bodies that we naturally are retracting and molding into a fetal position. We may tend to bend our legs into our chest while sitting, our shoulders may be raised toward the ears, our arms naturally cross over our chest, and our whole body curves and contracts. The fetal position is a defensive position—it allows us to shield ourselves from perceived ongoing attacks. We also do this energetically, creating a pattern in which our energy field is very close to our physical body and in which we mentally create all sorts of armoring. This energetic shielding is often unconscious, and has been done because the sensitive or psychic is in a state of overwhelm and protecting themselves the best way that they currently know how.

One of the easiest methods of shielding is to cross our arms and legs and move into fetal position. This allows us to stop energy or shield ourselves from having energy move into our physical body when we feel unprotected. Shielding naturally blocks energy from coming into us, but can be perceived as defensive (and rightfully so) by the people with whom we are interacting.

While shielding can be beneficial, and is in fact a crucial skill to learn, when a psychic continually blocks off and closes down their field, as well as their physical body, it is quite detrimental. Creating a closed energy field requires a great deal of energy and is the reason why many unskilled psychics are chronically fatigued and have amped-up nervous systems as well as subsequent health issues. The combination of a hypervigilant nervous system and the amount of energy needed to continually create rigid boundaries results not only in fatigue but issues with the immune system and the other physiological systems. To remain healthy, they require energy and a balanced state of interaction within the system, as well as between the individual and their environment.

The manner in which the psychic blocks, armors, or shields continually has major emotional and interpersonal repercussions. When we are closed off like this we do not have a natural flow to our lives. We are constantly guarded and on high alert, scanning the room and the people in it. This causes people to perceive us as having low effect or of being not available for friendships and relationships. A natural exchange of energies is intended to happen between people, between ourselves and the environment, which does not happen with such rigid boundaries. This has an isolating effect on the psychic, who does not understand that their overly rigid boundaries are causing them to not interact with people, to flow with people and environments, in the way they should.

If we lack boundaries, or have boundaries that are too wide, we can also have a great deal of difficulty. Because we do not have healthy boundaries, many people may notice this and take advantage of us.

To help with this we will discuss Energy Field Expansion, a technique that allows us to spread our energy field as wide as the entire world if not the universe. This technique is carried out in a highly skilled state and is beneficial to many psychics. But when we are unskilled and our boundaries are really wide (if we have boundaries at all) we do not retain a sense of individual self. This means that we may have no concept of who we are as people and completely lack embodiment.

When we lack boundaries, we may not understand who we are. We are constantly in a sea of stimuli and find ourselves changing and shifting based on our environment and the people we are around. When we lack boundaries we are constantly picking up the emotions, thoughts, and even the physical illnesses of people around us. In an unskilled state, this means that we are constantly on a roller coaster of emotions and various physical pains and complaints, typically without understanding that these emotions and experiences are not our own. In addition we are in a sea of thoughts, and we may be picking up on thoughts and experiencing them as our own without knowing it.

By developing boundaries in a healthy way we can learn how to have more balanced relationships, as well as become skilled at navigating times when we need to protect ourselves by "sealing of the aura" or when we may need to work with actually expanding ourselves.

Generally, as we get healthier and learn how to use the skills in the Basic Skills and Intermediate Skills chapters, we find that, in all but certain cases, expansion is the healthier option. As we grow healthier and more skilled, tools like Shielding become less dominant as we learn how to open more and to seal properly. Except in emergency situations, shutting ourselves down in any way as psychics is something that is necessary to know how to do (and do properly), but in most cases is not something that should be done on a regular basis.

Energy Field Expansion and Release

Most psychics have a really wide but unbalanced field. This means quite simply that it has gaps in it, places where emotions and energies from the outside world come in. In time, the typical psychic either subconsciously (or very consciously) creates a shield, or brings their energy really close in to their body to protect themselves. If we shield on a regular basis it depletes our energy.

If we do not have a wide field, we will feel invisible in our own lives, or lack the vital energy as well as willingness to interact with the outer world. Even if we are the most highly sensitive person who ever lived, we must have connections with other people, with nature, with animals, and with the world in order to be healthy mentally, emotionally, and spiritually. Without these connections we lose our health, our physical stamina, and retreat within ourselves, hiding from the outer world.

The healthiest energy field is one that is strong, vibrant, exchanges energy readily, and does not have any gaps in it. The more we use the other skills in this book, the more we will not only have a balanced energy field but will recognize when we get off balance and have methods to correct it.

Although some of this advice will be thought of as commonplace, it is important for the sensitive or psychic to expand their energy field and release energy from it on a regular basis. The best way to release energy from the physical body and energy field is through exercise. It does not have to be vigorous exercise—a simple walk in the park can be enormously effective.

Moving exercise, such as yoga, tai chi, qi gong, or martial arts, can teach the psychic how to release energy, emotions, and maintain the integrity and balance of their whole system. This is true even if your teacher has no clue what an "energy field" is, or what psychic abilities or sensitivities are.

One of the biggest energetic and spiritual releases from the body is through the pores of our skin. By sweating we release, and when we release (physically, emotionally, and energetically) we are not only maintaining our physical health but also our energetic and spiritual health. We are also expanding our energy field in a positive and vibrant way.

The more we learn to expand our energy field—and physical exercise is the easiest way to do this—and release that which is not serving us, or that which is not ours in the first place, the healthier and more functional we become. Many of us may not realize that having a healthy physical body is linked to our spiritual nature. But all aspects of ourselves are on a continuum. Our spiritual nature informs our physical nature, and our physical body informs our spiritual nature. By achieving health in many areas, not just spiritually, we can truly become balanced, happy, and healthy as psychics living in this world.

In this state of looking for balance we may find that our mental constructs need to change, and that we not only need to become healthy physically and spiritually by learning the tools in this book but that our mental outlook, beliefs, and thoughts need to change. Although it often is a tough sell, learning a simple meditation and maintaining a regular practice of daily meditation is crucial for any psychic. There are many different types of meditations out there, from quite simple and nondogmatic to very esoteric. There is a meditation type, style, and length that is perfect for you.

In finding a meditation practice, remember that simplicity is best. A highly charged and difficult meditation to open your crown chakra is not advised, as that can put someone who is naturally sensitive into a state of emergency. If you focus on stress relief, grounding, and simplicity (such as the basic *Tree* meditation), even for five minutes a day, you will begin to feel much healthier.

When we take care of our physical body, our thoughts, and our spiritual nature, we can truly come into a state of balance. The exercise below will teach you how to expand and release from your energy field.

Although the natural methods of exercising and meditation are wonderful to release and expand our energy field regularly, it is through knowing what our own energy field feels like or looks like to us, as well as acquiring the skills, confidence, and experience in doing so, that we can really begin to understand what or who is in our personal space.

As mentioned, our energy field is the area around us. Generally speaking, we have four energy "bodies" separate from the physical. The nearest to the physical body is the *etheric*, followed by the *astral* body. Beyond these are the *mental* and *spiritual* bodies. Working with the mental and spiritual bodies is very advanced work, and to get out of the cycle of overwhelm that many psychics are in, learning to work with the etheric and astral first is of the utmost importance before moving on. For the sake of simplicity, we will be working with the first two layers: the etheric and astral bodies.

Working with the Etheric Body

Moving out from the physical body, the etheric body is the first energetic body we encounter. It is roughly the same shape as our human form (which is why in some schools of thought it is considered our "double") but just beyond our physical body, approximately 3-6 inches on average.

How far your etheric body is from the confines of your physical body depends on your energy field as a whole. If you are someone who tends to retract their energy due to overwhelm or an innate need for protection, all of your bodies, including your etheric, will move in closer. If you are feeling wonderful, such as after exercise, sex, or just having a good day, your energy bodies will become more open and move farther away from you.

As was mentioned previously, a healthy energy body is open and is regularly exchanging energy with its environment. This is considered a state of free flow, where we are able to have the largest energies (even huge energies from the world or the cosmos) move through us without being affected. This takes a lot of work and patience to achieve, but if we begin to learn and practice the tools in this book, we can move closer to that state.

If we are open, and our energy is flowing both in and out, cycling through us in a healthy way, we will not have energies "stick" to us that cause us harm. Although we are talking about opening these bodies, being open does not mean that we lack boundaries, lose our identity, or let others take advantage of us. Instead, the state of being open allows us to eventually move into a state of noticing rather than reaction. By learning how to open ourselves, rather than retract, shield, or protect, we can learn to have both good and bad flow through us—the "bad" flowing through us and leaving, and the "good" flowing to us and through us, so that our lives can change for the better.

Many unskilled psychics, as we have discussed, block and shield themselves, retreating from not only the perceived negative but also the positive. As a result, they eventually report physical symptoms such as fatigue and overwhelm as well as a sense of being stuck and not moving forward in their lives. This is the effect of closing ourselves off to energy. The skilled thing to do is to learn how to open and expand these bodies, and to begin to discern when we may need to use other skills on occasion, such as sealing and shielding.

EXERCISE: Expanding the Etheric Body

To find where your etheric body is, you will do the following:
- Put your hands on your shoulders, palms out.
- Now you are going to lightly push out until you feel like you either meet a barrier or your hands feel like they are hesitating for some reason.

This is how you find your etheric body. If you do not have energy work training, it is easy to push past this barrier. If you do so, you will simply go back to your shoulders and try again, remembering that for most people the edge of the etheric body is approximately 3-6 inches away. In rare cases, people may find that they are not able to find their etheric body because they have no boundaries. If this is the case, working for a while with the Energetic Hygiene chapters, as well as some of the tools in the Basic Skills and Intermediate Skills chapters over a period of time will calm your system down enough to bring back in your energy so you can accomplish this exercise.

When you find the etheric body, visualize or sense what you notice about it. For example, most people notice that this body is dark or gray, but there are variations on this. Instead of automatically seeing what others tell you to be true, any psychic should begin to build their own library of experiences. This means that although it is widely taught and experienced that the etheric body is grayish and takes the shape of the human form (its double), you may experience it differently. It is okay to have experiences and insights that are from your own "library" rather than what is commonly taught. With time, you will build a library of understandings from your own direct experiences, which is important to become a skilled psychic rather than simply parroting what you have been taught by others.

Allow your focus to go to the etheric body—whatever you can sense of it. If you need to push your hands out again to discover its boundaries, that's fine. The next time you push your hands out (moving from the shoulders outward), inhale and push the edge of the boundary of your etheric body slightly outward as you exhale. You do not need to push it far. Listen to your intuition about where this body should be, what would be a balanced state for you—more open but not so open that it creates fear or overwhelm for you.

This exercise can be repeated on a daily basis, and it is interesting to track how you might be feeling that day and where this body is. Chances are that in time you will begin to notice that when you are not feeling well or are overwhelmed you close and retract this body. When you begin to notice this (and are ready), you can again take a breath and push this energy field out, dispersing energy rather than retracting it. When you begin to realize that retracting actually shuts in the energy (whatever stimulus you are reacting to), the idea of opening more to "vent" will sound more appealing. But for now, simply move at your own pace, and allow your intuition to guide you in expanding the etheric body outward.

Working with the Astral Body

Moving outward, the astral body is the next energetic body after we encounter the etheric body. To find the astral you will use the same procedure as you did with the etheric body, except this time you are looking for the second barrier rather than the first. In most people this barrier is 6-12 inches away from the physical body. This again can vary based on a number of factors. The astral body is our emotional body, and so it is often viewed in colors. True clairvoyants are able to see this body and associate the colors, clouds, faces, and stamps-type energies that appear with how people are doing and what sort of energy that individual people carry with them.

Even if you are not a highly trained clairvoyant, the astral body is most commonly associated with color, and the first color commonly seen is the color blue. As with the last exercise, you are encouraged to have direct experiences of your own, and to develop confidence in your own library of experiences over time.

EXERCISE: Expanding the Astral Body

As with the etheric body, you will find the barrier, inhale, then exhale, pushing the barrier of the astral body outward as far as is comfortable. When people begin to work with this body they may feel emotion releasing. This is actually a good thing, as we are developing a pathway outward for trapped emotions that were residing within us. Both the etheric and astral energy bodies can be expanded until they feel in a comfortable place for you. They do take a bit of time to work with, but understanding how to expand rather than retract, which is the natural inclination of the psychic, will allow you to stop the cycle of energetic retraction and creating harm for yourself. By expanding instead of retracting, or closing down, we are no longer in defense mode and allow things to flow through us, instead of sticking inside us.

Working on expanding rather than retracting our energy bodies can truly have a huge impact on our lives. We will find ourselves more joyous, more in the flow, with more opportunities coming our way. This of course takes some time, but it is the trait of an expanded field (which will happen by doing these exercises) that more joy, more health, more opportunities, and more balance come into our lives.

Sealing the Aura

Although it may seem contrary to talk about sealing after working with expansion, it is important to understand that sealing and shielding are two completely different mechanisms. We often think in black-or-white sorts of measures, wanting to completely shield ourselves or completely open ourselves. If, instead we think about being as open as is healthy for us, and how to seal instead of shield, we can come into a healthy state of balance and energetic dynamics. This will allow us to be open and able to establish appropriate boundaries for energies (and people) that require such boundaries.

Sealing allows us to create an energetic mechanism that keeps specific energies at bay. It is different from shielding, which generally closes down an area and keeps all energy out. When we seal we can introduce specific variables, such as the amount of time that the seal will remain, as well as what type of energy is to be kept out. I suggest you take the time to carry out sealing every morning if you are in a state of overwhelm, if you work with clients or the general public, or if you are going into a difficult environment such as a family gathering, bar, hospital, or grocery store.

EXERCISE: Sealing the Aura

To seal your aura, we will again be beginning with the outer layer, the astral body, which we discovered in the previous exercises. Find that boundary again through pushing your hands outward. You can also choose to open the etheric and astral bodies first, meaning that those boundaries will have expanded to what feels comfortable to you, before doing your sealing work.

You will then imagine sunlight coming from the outside in. In many cultures the sun is considered to be divine energy, and it is important in creating your seal that this energy come from the outside in (and you are not creating this energy and pushing it outward, which can be depleting). This sunlight will come around the boundary of the astral body and envelop it. See, sense, or feel this to whatever extent you are able to. Some people, especially when beginning, will benefit by actually doing this exercise in sunlight so that they can more readily feel and sense it enveloping them.

At this point, tell the sunlight how long you wish the seal to remain there (if you have not done this before, four hours or less is suggested—longer as you build upon this exercise) and if there is a specific type of energy you wish to keep out. If you would like to keep things general, you will simply ask for any energies that will not be of benefit to you to be dissolved in the sunlight, and any energies that would be of benefit to you to come through the sunlight and be filtered down to you. You will then say a simple "thank you" and go about your day.

Sealing the Physical Body

Although this is common knowledge, our physical body ends at the skin layer. Our pores are one of the best energy releasers and clearers of not only the physical energies but also spiritual energies. In most cases, sealing the aura is all that people need to do. It provides enough protection and is enough of a barrier that with practice it becomes strong enough to dissolve even the most difficult of energies.

However, there are some situations that call for a step beyond the sealing of the aura. We may feel like we are in physical peril, or are exhausted, depleted, or are in a dangerous situation. Sealing the physical body is suggested for most psychics who visit graveyards, hospitals, warehouse stores, battle sites (even if the battle has long past), and areas that have significant negative energy. Some psychics have a tremendous amount of difficulty with sleep, such as strange dreams, nightmares, or even being attacked or sensing strange presences in the room. For people who feel some element of danger, sealing the physical body is helpful in keeping energies away.

Due to the nature of this exercise, I caution people who have issues with anxiety, claustrophobia, or heart-related issues to use this tool with care. Whenever you use it, it is a good idea to check in with how you are feeling about half an hour later. If you are experiencing any difficulty, such as feeling anxious, releasing the body seal is a good idea.

EXERCISE: Sealing the Physical Body

To begin sealing the physical body, first make contact with the skin layer of your body. This can be done by brushing upward on your forearm with your opposite hand.

Then begin to become aware of the skin throughout your body. Do this by performing a simple body scan, starting at the feet and moving up the body. The skin is like a container, or a sort of sock. Physically, we are composed of skin and fascia (the underlying densely woven tissue) that create our basic human form. This is all connected, and with focus, some of us are able to sense our skin, fascia, and the other components that create our basic outer shape.

The fascia and skin form a sort of woven matrix, or spider web, throughout our body. This matrix not only facilitates physical but also energetic exchanges. Imagine, sense, feel this spider web throughout your body. Now you will ask this spider web to become denser and more fibrous, pulling closer together. You will still want a bit of space for physical and energetic exchange of energies, but you can close it, reweave it, or allow it to become thicker and tighter. Some will picture this as metallic wiring, or something more protective than woven tissue.

You will again ask for a specific amount of time for this to occur, such as a few hours, and intend that specific energies not be allowed in. In most cases, it works to ask that generally positive, or helpful, energies be allowed through and negative, or harmful, energies be stopped by the woven matrix. If you would like to seal multiple "bodies," you will seal the astral first before sealing the physical.

NOTE: When you work with sealing, or reweaving, the physical body, you will want to remain awake or conscious of what is going on for the next 20 minutes or so. This is not to cause fear or alarm about this exercise, which is generally safe and very helpful, but to consider that some people react to sealing the physical body with anxiety. If this happens, go back in and loosen the wires or threads (by imagining this happening and asking the skin/fascia to do so), or dissolve it completely by allowing the sun from the astral layer of protection to dissolve it—both are effective means of reversing the sealing work.

These seals are best done over a period of time. This means that the first time we create a seal, it may be very effective and quite strong. But the fiftieth time we do so, we are likely not to have to exert much if any effort, and it will be much stronger and resilient naturally.

By working with both expanding as well as sealing the energy and physical bodies (and yes, expanding and then sealing can be done together), the appropriate energy dynamics that are right for you will begin to form and strengthen. This will allow you to go into even the most negative or difficult situations and come out without feeling depleted, harmed, or even off balance.

Shielding

If you employ the skills in the previous sections of the book appropriately, it will all but stop the need for conscious shielding. Learning how to seal, rather than shield, is highly effective and does not create any damage to the energy systems of the body. That being said, we are not all to the point of being skilled enough to have a healthy, balanced system that naturally wards off detrimental energies that may come our way.

EXERCISE: Shield

The easiest method of shielding is to work with the last exercise in this book—Heart Space Radiance—and aim the energy developed through that exercise at a piece of clothing or an item of jewelry that you wear frequently. Choose a piece of clothing or a necklace that you feel really strong, really yourself wearing. It is likely a piece of clothing, necklace, coat, or other accessory that you get compliments on, or simply feel really good wearing. It should be something that you wish to wear frequently.

Choose a day that you are feeling really strong and healthy. If you never have those days, simply do the best you can and choose a day that you feel pretty strong. You could also visit an energy worker or spiritual healer you trust and ask them to create this clothing shield for you. You will expand your energy field (your etheric and astral bodies) and then do the *Heart Space Radiance* exercise at the end of this chapter. Hold the object, allowing your heart space radiance to emanate into the object. Then ask that sunlight (see the Astral Body section) flow into the object from the outside in. These two energies (heart radiance and sunlight) will combine in the object.

As this is happening, whisper "No harm may come to me" into the object as many times as feels appropriate. The object should start to feel warm, or have a felt sense or visual sense of being empowered or "alive." This object is now programmed to keep you safe. Any time you are feeling physically healthy, or are able to, you can add to this programming by doing the same procedure. If you go to a spiritual healer or energy worker, ask how often you should reprogram the object.

You can now wear this object on a regular basis, or whenever you feel that harm may come your way. Come up with a phrase that is appropriate for your own life, but it should be simple and whispered into the object in the same manner. By programming an object or article of clothing, you are shielding yourself in a manner that does not cause you energetic harm. Most people create shields within or around themselves using aspects of their physical body and their own energy, which is depleting and causes problems over time, especially if they forget they have shielded themselves, or have done so on a subconscious level.

EXERCISE: Full Energy Blocking Shield

The other method of shielding is a last resort, but as this is a book teaching essential skills for psychics, it should be included. This method of shielding uses your own energy and blocks all energy, good and bad, basically stopping any sort of energetic exchange. It is appropriate for emergency situations, and all skilled psychics should know how to erect a proper shield.

NOTE, however, that even in the worst sort of energetic environment, if you have learned and practiced the tools described in detail in the previous chapters of the book, you are more likely to come out unscathed.

To erect a shield, first create a strong emotion within yourself. If you are in a difficult situation, you are likely fearful, but you might want to call up anger (which makes a wonderful shield) if that is within you.

Focus on this emotion, and ask it to build within you. This is not so that you explode on the nearest passerby, or in traffic, but so that you can build enough energy to create an effective shield.

Once you have felt this energy build, imagine it as a color. Black is generally suggested for fear, red for anger. Visualize or sense this anger emanating from you into a single point in front of you. Let it form a ball of colored energy. Keep on releasing your energy (the emotion) into the ball. As you do so, ask it to form a shield, a protective layer surrounding you.

Watch or sense as it comes into that shape. Let it know what it is to shield you from and how long you would like it to be there. If you would just like to be shielded from negative energy, in general, you can simply state that. When you are doing this, please let it know how long it should remain, otherwise you are likely to forget about it once you are out of the difficult situation.

The energetics of this shield are simple. You are projecting your strong energy (the emotion) forward in a protective manner. Anything that comes across this projected energy is likely to react to the emotion and energy you have projected. Simply put, in a schoolyard a bully is likely to pick on someone who has no defenses, not someone who is radiating a shield around them.

It should be noted that one of the difficulties of this shield is that interpersonal energies get a bit askew. We all react to subconscious impressions of people, psychic or not, so if you are shielding with projected anger or fear, it is likely that people are going to sense it on some level. This may be exactly what you want, by the way, but it may not be the best thing to do before a job interview or in a place where you will need to interact cheerfully with a lot of other people.

In general, shields are not suggested, because to be effective they use your own energy. It is normal to feel tired after projecting your own emotions forward, or even your mental energies. Many other books work with mental energies to create shields, and while some of them are moderately effective, working with emotions is much more effective. Even more effective is to become skilled, balanced, and clear enough to never need to shield at all.

Words of Power

Words are things, and the way that we speak and the manner in which we articulate what we want, as well as our general conviction in doing so, can allow us to more readily receive what we want in this world.

What this means is that if we are meekly creating a shield and stating our intent with a quivering voice, it is much less likely to be effective than if we were to create our shield with confidence and a loud, booming voice. If we approach a situation with confidence (even if we are uncertain if we are doing a skill as well as we likely will in the future after practice), we are more likely to have more positive results.

This also means that the more specific we are with our words, or our intent, the more realized it will become. Words have power. Our presence has power. The more that we can stand in our power and clearly state our intent the more powerful we become, and the easier it is to cleanse, clear, protect, and shield ourselves and our homes. This also extends to the outer world; when we are capable of stating what we want in this world, clearly and directly, we are opening ourselves up energetically to receive it.

This technique can be used to great effect with shielding, spiritual bathing, house clearing, as well as working with many other types of situations. When you are using the techniques already described (such as spiritual bathing, clearing your home, or creating a shield) I would like you to come up with a simple phrase that you will use every single time you do so, no matter what the situation is. It is best if this phrase is simple, direct, and focused.

For example, for a shield you may wish to say:

> This shield will protect me from negative thoughts, emotions, and any negative energies that come my way for the next three hours.

For clearing a house you may say something such as:

> I give thanks to those who help and surround me. I give thanks to my god who protects me. Let this room be clear of any negative energies, spirits, beings, or heavy energy.

It is important that you create your own phrases to be used, with your own concept of faith or spiritual path as a part of the saying. The saying can be quite simple, and may be added on to when a situation warrants it. By developing this phrase or simple sentence, and repeatedly using it, you are shifting into a higher consciousness, or "powering up," with the repetition of the words you develop becoming a power all their own. Over time, the words and phrases that you use will become more and more powerful, as well as more effective.

Warding

Warding is a way to add another layer of protection to your home, living space, and land. You may wish to ward your home so that no negative energies come through, or no energies at all come through unless they are specifically invited.

Warding can get quite complex and technical, but simplicity as well as focus while warding is quite effective as an extra safety mechanism. Most people, unless they are doing spiritual work or energy work on their property, will not need anything beyond the simple warding procedure detailed below.

EXERCISE: Warding

> To ward, you will first want to clear your space as was taught in the "House Clearing" section. This is to clear energies, so that you have less of a chance of "locking" energies in by putting a ward around your home while there are still energies around and within your home.
>
> After you have cleared your home, you will get four rocks or four crystals of equal size (about fist size, although they can be smaller or larger). You will not want these to be expensive objects, because you will be placing them around your property or possibly even burying them. If you do not have rocks or crystals, you can also use dirt from the four corners of your property.
>
> When you find the objects, you will want to clear them. You can do so with salt water or by using the "Heart Space Radiance" energy cultivation and imagining the energy emanating into the objects. The purpose in clearing the object is not so that it becomes a blank slate but to remove any excess energies, so that the essence, or natural properties, of the object can be restored.
>
> You now will use "Words of Power" with a specific, short intent, such as "You will protect my property from any negative or heavy energies," or "My house will be protected from anything that wishes me or my family harm." Or even simpler, you can just whisper the word "protect" repeatedly to the object. To do this, you will pick up

each rock or crystal and whisper the intent to the object until there is a subtle change felt in the object. This may take a bit of time to cultivate, but is quite noticeable when done correctly. You will do this for each rock until you feel this subtle change for each one, and then will do the same for all four grouped together. If you are working with dirt, you will stick your fingers into the dirt and whisper the intent to the dirt after mixing together the four corners dirt you have gathered.

You will then bury or place the rocks at the corners of your property. If you are in an apartment or similar space you can put these objects in the inner corner of each room. If you do this procedure correctly, you will sense or feel a distinct barrier form when all four rocks or crystals are buried or placed. If you are working with dirt, you would bring a quarter of the mixture to the four corners of your land, or sprinkle a fourth of the dirt in each corner of your home or room that you wish to ward.

Over time, the ward will naturally dissipate. For beginners, warding once a week is suggested. When you build up power and become more accustomed to working like this it is likely that you will get an intuitive sense about when to re-ward the property. Once a month at minimum is suggested, if you use this method.

When redoing this method on subsequent occasions, you can use the same rocks or crystals, if you can find them. You do not need to clear them again, and can just move on to the intent or "Words of Power" portion of working with each rock. If you are unable to find the rocks or crystals, or are working with dirt, know that the ward will naturally dissipate and you can use new materials to ward, again going through the whole procedure detailed above.

Moving Beyond Fear/Non-Reaction

It is part of our natural defense system to have a lot of fear about the unknown, or about spiritual stimuli coming at us. It is even easier to shield, protect ourselves, or create a situation in which we constantly believe that we are under attack.

Many psychics have an adversarial relationship with the spirit world because they consistently feel like they are being cursed, punished, or simply overstimulated by having so much information come at them that other people do not have to deal with. This is especially true for moderately and highly psychic individuals, who are often so in tune that it is like watching five, ten, or fifty televisions at the same time. With that much stimuli coming at them, it is typical for the psychic to feel constantly overwhelmed and in a state of fear. As we have seen, much of this fear can be addressed using the skills listed throughout this book. When we feel more in control of our abilities, understand them, and know how to use them, we come out of the sympathetic shock, or "fight or flight" syndrome, that many of us are in and can realize a state of balance.

It sounds almost too easy to say that psychics should go to a state of noticing rather than reaction to stimuli coming their way. This is taught in many mainstream circles through meditations and understandings that make it seem like we should have no emotions whatsoever—as if we should be dead from the neck down. But we are intended to have emotions, we are intended to have reactions, and we are intended to interact with our environment in a way in which we are exchanging energy with it. If we are not exchanging energy with other people and places it is easy for the psychic to get depleted, feel isolated, lost, and not connected. This exchange of energies is important for physical and psychic health.

But in many cases we overreact. We have been in a state of fear, of overwhelm, so long that any stimuli coming our way cause us to react in a more magnified way than the situation calls for.

Picture this: two women get into the same type of car accident at different times. The first is annoyed but goes through calling her insurance agency, getting her car towed, and booking a massage in order to release any issues associated with the accident. She is slightly shaken throughout the next day or two but lets go of the experience and only begins to think about it when she has to do things like call her mechanic.

The second gets into the same accident and a well of rage streams up in her, and she becomes angry and screams at the other person involved in the collision. Her entire body begins to shake, and she feels enormous amounts of fear, rage, and overwhelm. She develops a migraine and then has to go to bed for three days after the incident because of exhaustion and head pain.

Although these are simplified examples, familiar to anyone in the general population and not just people who are considered "sensitive," they are apt for the psychic and sensitive community. If we have a backlog of overwhelm or reactions to past events, current events will be magnified. Put more simply: if we have not worked through the massive amounts of anger or fear from our past, it will still affect us in the present. If we have a backlog of unprocessed anger, when we are put into a situation in which we appropriately become angry or irritated (such as getting into a car accident), our anger will be magnified.

The same is true of overwhelm. If we are sensitive to the extent that we are overwhelmed, a trip to a place that is difficult for many people—such as the grocery store or hospital—is a magnified experience for the psychic, creating a state of exhaustion in them whereas someone else may simply feel a bit tired or feel fine after their trip to those same places.

So what does all of this mean? The process of nonreaction, or moving beyond fear, is a conscious one. This means that we can recognize that when we get angry, feel fear, or experience overwhelm that our experiences may be being magnified. This is not to blame the psychic for having these backlogged emotions and experiences, but to consciously realize how magnified they may be.

When we are able to consciously realize this type of information, we naturally begin to take personal responsibility for it. If we are overwhelmed and respond to a task such as replying to an email or doing laundry as if it were a Herculean undertaking, we can realize what is happening, and take responsibility for doing whatever activities are needed for us to come out of overwhelm.

Similarly with emotions, if we find ourselves reacting to a situation with more anger than the situation warrants, we can find time or resources, such as meditation, exercising, yoga, or talk therapy, to release our anger and any other backlogged emotions and experiences we may have.

We return to the subject of fear. It is natural for many of us to feel overwhelmed and fearful as a part of reacting to spiritual stimuli. Anything that would be considered "spiritual"—meaning not a concrete part of our reality that most people would agree upon—is something to be afraid of.

With skill and understanding this fear will dissipate. But we can also work with fear, overwhelm, and any other emotions in the following way:

- The next time you react to a situation, consider what emotion or emotions you are feeling (anger, fear, grief, numbness, overwhelm).
- Consider what part of this reaction was appropriate. By this, I mean that if you work a 12-hour shift, it is appropriate to feel tired. If someone causes you to get in a car accident, it is natural to

feel angry. If someone mugs or assaults you, it is appropriate to feel fear.

- Now consider how much of this reaction was magnified. You can do simple percentages here (10 percent was appropriate, 90 percent was magnified), or you may wish to state that your fear was magnified 5, 10, or 20 times more than it should have been.
- State this percentage back to yourself again, and give yourself permission to fully feel the appropriate emotion or experience. Often we do not give ourselves permission to feel any emotions, but if we do not do so, they just get added on to the stockpile for next time,
- Consider what activity is needed for the backlogged information, such as rest or meditation for exhaustion, exercise to release emotions, and so forth.

As you do this more you will realize that you are not reacting the way you did in the past. By making this process conscious, as well as learning the appropriate tools for how to work with your sensitivities, you will become aware of the backlogged material. This activity pairs really well with the *Calibrating Energy* exercise in the previous chapter, and if both are done regularly you can come to a state of noticing and a state of appropriate reaction.

One of my teachers used to always state that even in the most dire of spiritual situations, minimal or no reaction to what is in front of you is the best defense. Even in the worst sorts of spiritual warfare, or the relative who consistently belittles and provokes you at family gatherings, these energies and people are looking for an emotional reaction. By fully taking responsibility for not only understanding who the person is (calibrating energy) but also your own reactions (this exercise), you will not only have better interactions with those around you, and the world in general, but you will likely find over time that those who are looking for these types of reactions simply find someone else to provoke.

In the case of spiritual overwhelm and fear, the more we find stability, understanding, and develop healthy boundaries and skills with our abilities, the less fear and overwhelm we will have, and the less we will react to the spiritual realms as a fearful place, or our lives through the lens of constantly being too overwhelmed to function appropriately in them.

Heart Space Radiance

Although this book has focused to a larger extent on how a psychic can develop the skills to protect themselves, all of which are necessary tools, we may find as we progress that instead of blocking, stopping, or controlling our abilities, we may wish to come from a place of ease and openness with them.

All skilled psychics know how to work with their abilities, how to maintain energetic hygiene, boundaries, and protect themselves, when necessary. But when we do work with these skills, we may find that the greatest skill, the most wonderful tool we can cultivate is that of compassion and light in our heart.

As I write this, I realize that this understanding is often skewed by modern spiritual circles, and that the sort of "Love is all we need" mentality that is often popularized with the best of intentions often simply doesn't work for psychics who are struggling—and certainly does not work for psychics at all points in their lives. So there is a very real need for understanding how to protect, how to close, how to seal. This information can truly be life-saving.

But as we find ourselves considering our abilities, and reconcile the parts of ourselves that are overwhelmed, afraid, and struggling, it is an ideal time to move into knowing how to cultivate the heart space. This space and its radiance are really the best defense for most situations. By cultivating this space, we become more at peace within ourselves, and this peace emanates from us, transforming whatever we come across.

When we are feeling overwhelmed or simply having an "off" day, it is natural to lose track of ourselves and go into a place of feeling like the world and the people inhabiting it are filled with darkness. By focusing on compassion and inner work with the heart, we can find ourselves stepping out of this perspective and embracing the positive aspects of our abilities, as well as feeling better in general about the world and the people in it.

Before we begin, it is important to understand that no matter how lost, traumatized, upset, or out of balance we may be, we all have the spark of divinity within us, and it is contained in our heart. It is the true essence of who we are, and allows us to feel compassion not only for the world but also ourselves. By activating and working with this light, making it more radiant, we truly change how we react to our abilities as well as how we manifest in the world.

MEDITATION: Heart Radiance

- First, feel your heart space in the center of your chest. How does it feel to you? Tight, heavy, light, joyful, sad, chaotic, peaceful?
- Now look a bit deeper to see a spark of light. This may be the first time you have ever done this, so this light may be quite small.
- If you are unable to see or sense this spark, ask yourself, "What would happen if I were able to see or sense this spark?"
- When you notice it, simply sit with it for a moment and notice how it makes you feel.
- When you are ready, you will ask this spark to grow larger and brighter.
- Allow it to naturally grow as much as it is able to. You do not need to force anything.
- Each time you return, notice this spark and ask it to grow larger and brighter.

When it feels like this light has grown to the point that it is bright and emanating from you past your physical body, you can continue. The next step is to use this in your daily life:

- When you are noticing a source or issue that is bothering you, check in with your heart spark and allow this radiance to flow toward the person or situation that is causing you difficulty.
- When you are feeling fear or overwhelm, allow yourself to access this spark and grow it until it radiates from you. It will naturally settle the fear and overwhelm.
- If you are in a situation that is causing you to feel attacked, build up this heart space radiance as large as you are able to. Allow it to envelop you.

By beginning to react with this radiance instead of fear or protection, we can eventually learn to clear many of the most difficult stimuli and situations that surround us and overwhelm us. We can go from coming across another person who is angry and afraid, and us reacting by taking on that anger or fear and protecting ourselves, to developing healthy boundaries and calibrating, to eventually developing our heart space radiance to the point that we simply notice the anger and fear emanating from the other person and feel compassion for them. It must be difficult for that person to feel anger and fear, or to want to attack other people (energetically or otherwise).

By developing this radiance when we go into difficult situations, such as family gatherings, bars, hospitals, and other places, we step into a different vibration, which prevents difficult or negative energies from our environments from sticking to us in the way they used to do.

There are some incredibly difficult spaces out there, and a psychic should always practice energetic hygiene before, during, and after engaging with these situations, as well as seal, shield, and protect themselves, when necessary. This is why it is important for psychics to have a wide variety of tools and skills, so that we can go into a situation with a cultivated heart space when we are able to, or we can determine that what we really need to do is to shield or protect ourselves. By learning how to use all of the tools in this book over time, we can react appropriately to the situations around us, let go of overwhelm, understand our abilities, and thrive in a world that needs more real, compassionate, and skilled psychics.

Closing Thoughts and Advanced Work

As you go through this book, it is easy to become overwhelmed by the checklist of things suggested in order to become a skilled sensitive or psychic. You may look at a book like this, think about where you are in your life, and not feel like you can ever become a skilled psychic, or anywhere close to it.

But if you were to take just one skill and one exercise, such as the *Is This Mine?* exercise, and do it faithfully for a month, you would find yourself in a different and better place than you were before. None of us change overnight, or all at once. We change through titration—slowly allowing ourselves to come to realizations, developing new skills in order to become healthier and more functional in this world.

So I suggest that you do not work with everything in this book at once, but learn one skill, or two. Wait until they feel like second nature to you and become so easy that you no longer have to think about them, or only have to think about them in more difficult situations. This is what happens when you introduce any tool. At the beginning it is difficult, impossible even. We may be confused, frustrated, or feel as if we will never learn it. And then we realize a few weeks later, or a few months later, that we not only have learned it but that it is a completely natural impulse for us.

One question always comes up with sensitives and psychics: What to do about their sensitivities? This is an appropriate and completely natural question to have when someone looks out at the world and realizes that compared to most people they feel, sense, see, or hear more than others.

There may be a real spiritual path for you, a path in which you are directed to distinctly do something with your sensitivities. But simply because someone notices more than other people in a room doesn't mean that they need to do something about it. Whatever you are noticing—emotions, thoughts, spirits, and so forth—simply because you notice them, it does not mean that you have any sort of responsibility to them. This is similar to an architect who goes out and notices all of the different types of houses out there; they do not need to do anything about the fact that they can know which era each house they are noticing is from.

As sensitives and psychics, we tend to find ourselves taking responsibility for what we see and sense, and it's important to restate that we do not need to do this. This may seem crass to some psychics, because they tend to have the odd sense that because they know that a spirit is there they need to help the spirit, or the person it is attached to, or that they need to tell the person they are talking to their deeper truth or what is behind their mask. But if we were to let go of that responsibility, that feeling of because we are simply seeing or sensing more meaning that we are responsible for it, we would likely have much easier existences.

There is also a belief by sensitives and psychics that they cannot become functional due to their sensitivities. They exist in isolation, or blame their sensitivities for issues in their lives. No matter how sensitive we are, there is always someone more sensitive than we are. No matter how sensitive we are, we can learn tools to become healthy, functional human beings—people who can bring our unique sensitivities and gifts to a world that is hyper-focused on physical existence. Our capacity to feel, to sense, and to create can bring qualities to this world that are desperately needed. We just need to learn how to properly manage our abilities so that we can be that light to others.

So I want to reiterate that sensitives and psychics can bring a lot to this world, no matter in which capacity they choose to use their skills. They can deeply listen, understand, and see in a way that is rare in this world. They can make fabulous teachers, counselors, bodyworkers, energy workers, spiritual workers, architects, lawyers, police officers, entrepreneurs . . . the list goes on.

Our sensitivities and abilities are needed. The ability to look at situations more deeply or just differently can bring a lot to a world filled with people who are not sensing or feeling on the same level. Letting go of having to "do something" with our abilities and realizing how our individual path, whatever that may be, can allow our sensitivities to be an asset and allow us to be of service, without feeling as if we are responsible for everything we see or sense out there.

This book has taught you what you need to know to become functional in this world, to stop looking at your sensitivities as a detriment, and to learn how to work with them in an appropriate manner. If you have worked with the material fully, this book will have helped you to see your sensitivities as a source of strength rather than weakness, and given you the skills to stop reacting in a cycle of overwhelm. This will give you the confidence and skill required to know how to work with your individual psychic abilities and sensitivities to the point that you can be both sensitive or psychic as well as have a complex, complete, and fulfilling outer life complete with interacting with other people and the world.

As stated in the beginning, this is a book filled with skills, understandings, and exercises that can allow the unskilled psychic to become a skilled psychic. But it is also true that there is much more out there, and more skills to learn beyond this book.

So where do we go from here?

Some of you may choose to learn more skills and understandings to not only manage your psychic abilities but work with them further. The psychic or sensitive has a rare ability to work with spiritual helpers and ancestors, to develop a deep connection to themselves, and to connect uniquely and directly to divinity.

For those of you looking to do more advanced work, this would be the next step: to have real, direct connection to yourself and divinity. This book will certainly take you to that precipice, but there is a point where the sensitive or psychic has learned how to have control, to have skill, to manage their life, and now decides to move forward in embracing and loving their unique abilities and developing them as a source of strength in their lives. This is truly advanced work, and I hope that those of you who are looking for this realize that it is a possibility.

For all of you, I hope that, through working with the material in this book, you have realized that you can be psychic or sensitive and thrive in this world, and can bring your unique abilities as a source of strength into the world. This world desperately needs more sensitives and psychics who are real, who approach the world with humility and curiosity, who are willing to contribute to the world in a way that is real. For those of you willing to take that step, I commend you on your contributions, now and in the future.

About the Author

Mary Mueller Shutan is an Acupuncturist, CranioSacral Therapist, Zero Balancer, Herbalist, Spiritual Healer, and Artist. Through her own intense spiritual awakening process, she discovered simple, clear ways to help people with psychic abilities, kundalini, and other spiritual awakenings navigate their experiences. She has a worldwide practice and currently resides in Arizona.

Mary is the author of *The Spiritual Awakening Guide*, also published by Findhorn Press. For more information on her work please visit her website: *www.maryshutan.com*

Also of interest from Findhorn Press

The Spiritual Awakening Guide
by Mary Mueller Shutan

THIS PRACTICAL BOOK opens new understandings of how to live in the world while going through an awakening process. Mary Mueller Shutan provides tools for how to navigate through each of the twelve layers of an awakened state and explains how to recognize where we are in our spiritual journey, along with common physical, emotional, and spiritual symptoms that may be experienced on the way. She offers the revolutionary idea that we are meant to be humans, to have a physical body with physical, sensate experiences and emotions. We are meant to live in the world and be a part of it even as fully awakened individuals.

This guide proposes a look at the possibility of leading a grounded, earth-bound life of work, family, friends, and other experiences in an awakened state.

978-1-84409-671-8